WHITEHEAD AND JESUS

AN ADVENTURE IN SPIRITUAL TRANSFORMATION

BRUCE G. EPPERLY

I0148959

Energion Publications
Cantonment, Florida
2025

Cover Design: Henry Neufeld
Cover Image: Adobe Stock

ISBN: 978-1-63199-966-6
eISBN: 978-1-63199-967-3

Energion Publications
1241 Conference Rd
Cantonment, FL 32533

pubs@energion.com

TABLE OF CONTENTS

CHAPTER ONE

JUST A CLOSER WALK WITH THEE: A JOURNEY WITH WHITEHEAD AND JESUS

> *When the Pharisees heard that he had silenced the Sadducees, they gathered together, and one of them, an expert in the law, asked him a question to test him. "Teacher, which commandment in the law is the greatest?" He said to him, "You shall love the Lord your God with all your heart and with all your soul and with all your mind." This is the greatest and first commandment. And a second is like it: "You shall love your neighbor as yourself." (Matthew 22:34-39)*

> *The modern world has lost God and is seeking him…On the whole the gospel of Love was replaced by the gospel of fear. The Christian world was composed of terrified populations. If the modern world is to find God, it must find him through love and not fear with the help of John and not Paul.*[1]

This text charts a spiritual and theological journey, involving my personal relationship with Jesus of Nazareth and my equally personal and theological relationship with the philosopher Alfred North Whitehead. Both journeys, joined in tandem for over fifty years, have transformed and continue to transform my life. The contours of this text are, accordingly, both autobiographical and theological. Indeed, all authentic theology is grounded in the concreteness of our personal experiences of truth and error, faith and doubt, and infinity and finitude. Neither Jesus nor Whitehead isolated our spiritual lives from our world views and ethical commitments. We live in One World in which our ultimate allegiance to God shapes our economics, poli-

---

1   Alfred North Whitehead, *Religion in the Making* (New York: Meridian, 1960), 72-73.

tics, attitudes toward the non-human world, and personal lives and relationships. Our character is formed according to our most deeply held beliefs, according to Whitehead, and our most deeply held beliefs involve the dynamic interplay of spirituality and theology, as well as emotion and the intellect, and head, heart, and hands. The Word is made flesh in joining the Infinite and the Infinitesimal, and the Cosmic and the Personal. Jesus and Whitehead embody the Word and Wisdom of God made flesh in solitude and relationships for me: Jesus is my Teacher, Healer, Companion, and Guide; Whitehead is my Philosopher who, for me, best describes the contours of God's presence in our lives and the world.

I begin this text on Whitehead and Jesus with a confession: I am a cradle evangelical. In many ways, despite my progressive and universalist theological perspective as a process and open and relational theologian, I remain emotionally evangelical and mystical in orientation. Although I have journeyed far from my small-town evangelical roots, I still long for the day to day walk with God – and for experiencing a personal relationship with Jesus in times of joy and sorrow. The words of a childhood hymn are still my daily prayer, especially as I set out on my predawn walk:

> Just a closer walk with Thee,
> Grant it, Jesus, is my plea,
> Daily walking close to Thee,
> Let it be, dear Lord, let it be.[2]

I have heard the voice of God's Spirit and the challenging call of Jesus in the birds' morning melodies and in the wind whispering through the forest adjacent to our Potomac, Maryland, home. I have also heard God's call to companionship in the newsfeed headlines and the faces of immigrants and vulnerable children. When I ponder Whitehead's philosophical concept of God's initial aim, the divine possibility for meditated to each moment of experience, I think of

---

2   "Just a Closer Walk with Thee," author unknown.

the "still, small voice" of Divine Guidance and my memory returns
to another hymn I learned as a child, "In the Garden":

> He speaks, and the sound of His voice
> Is so sweet the birds hush their singing,
> And the melody that He gave to me
> Within my heart is ringing.
> And He walks with me, and He talks with me,
> And He tells me I am His own;
> And the joy we share as we tarry there,
> None other has ever known.[3]

When I pause in amazement at God's receptive and intimate love,
described theologically by Whitehead in terms of God's consequent
nature, what I describe as the Heart of the Universe, open to all our
joys and sorrows, and reflected in Jesus' companionship with his first
followers and in Christian experience throughout the centuries, my
memory returns to another evangelical hymn of childhood:

> What a friend we have in Jesus
> All our sins and griefs to bear.
> What a privilege to carry
> Everything to God in prayer.[4]

Whether mystical, evangelical, or progressive in theological orientation, we can affirm that God embraces every moment of joy and
sorrow. We can affirm God's companionship and guidance in every
moment of decision. God is the fellow sufferer who understands,
the constant presence who guides, and the joyful companion who
celebrates.

As a child I often experienced Jesus as near as my next breath. I
was my Baptist father's son and shared his deep faith in Jesus as our
Lord and Savior. I was an evangelical in spirit long before the term

---

3   C. Austin Miles, "In the Garden."
4   Joseph Scriven, "What a Friend We Have in Jesus."

was debased by its association with incivility, political idolatry, and white Christian nationalism. As a child, I heard the good news that "Jesus loves me, this I know, for the Bible tells me so." A pious Baptist child, I believed that what happened to me and my loved ones mattered to God and I prayed for everything from baseball games to issues involving my mother's mental health and the well-being of members of our church.

Long before I studied academic theology and philosophy, heard the word "Christology," or discovered the wisdom of Jewish mystic and theologian Abraham Joshua Heschel, I experienced God as alive and Jesus as personal, the "most moved mover," in contrast to the apathetic unmoved mover of Aristotle, described by many theologians as the model for divine perfection. Jesus was alive and his Spirit breathed in and through me, hearing my solitary evening prayers and intimately feeling my joy and sorrow.

At age nine, I "came forward" at an altar call, given by Leonard Eilers, evangelist to the Hollywood cowboy actors and stuntmen, whose traveling revival, "The Roundup for God," came to our church. I still remember the words of his theme song.

Put your foot in the stirrup
Climb up on the horse
The Roundup for God is on.

At age eleven, I lost my simple childhood faith. I experienced the spiritual upheavals of deconstruction long before the word became popular among ex-evangelicals to describe their exit from conservative and evangelical Christianity to agnosticism or a broader open and relational vision of faith. My father was dismissed from his Baptist pulpit, never to pastor a congregation again. Our family was forced to move from "idyllic" small town America to the fast-growing emerging Silicon Valley city of San Jose, California. In this new and diverse environment where church was an afterthought to our neighbors, I carried the grief of my temporarily impoverished family and disgraced and unemployed father. I came down with an undiagnosed illness, characterized by high temperature, listlessness, and hallucinations. After I recovered, I returned to church, a local Church of Christ, two blocks from our California tract home, because my father worked Sundays as a security guard in one of the first Silicon Valley semi-conductor plants. I belonged to the youth group for a year and excelled at Bible Drills, finding and reciting verses in record speed, but felt claustrophobic whenever I attended worship. My soul had departed from the conservative church and its ambiguous theological vision of God long before my body left. The intimate and personal Jesus was no longer near to me. I felt alone and spiritually rudderless, unable to join my experience of the loving Jesus with the demanding and punitive vision of God taught in the local church.

The year 1966 brought the Summer of Love to San Francisco, and within a year, I was immersed in the hippie movement, long hair, tie-dyed shirts, bell bottoms, a beard (once I could grow one!), and the magical mystery tour of marijuana, hashish, and psychedelics. I was on a spiritual quest and although I didn't identify this quest with Jesus, I wanted to experience God as personal again. My high school journey took me through American Transcendentalism, Buddhism, Hinduism, and Taoism. I read Alan Watts, Ram Dass, and Carlos Castaneda. Although I had ample options to take hard drugs such as cocaine and heroin, I believe that I was delivered from addiction because of my commitment to a hippie version of my childhood faith, the quest for a personal relationship with the Holy, a sense of nearness with the Spirit who gives life to all things. I flirted with the Jesus Movement, and enjoyed sharing conversations with long-haired Jesus freaks and their winsome pious girlfriends, but their joy in Jesus felt inauthentic to me. Beneath the joyful "isn't it cool that Jesus loves you," was an implicit fundamentalism and Christian exceptionalism that divided the world into the saved and unsaved, the heaven-bound and the eternally lost, and those who walked in light and the multitudes of faithful Buddhist, Hindus, Jews, and Muslims who stumbled in darkness. Eventually the Jesus Movement found its way to doctrinally narrow, rule oriented, and theologically inflexible churches like Calvary Chapel and was coopted by conservative Christianity and right-wing politics. I suspect many of today's MAGA-hatted Trump followers were once free-spirited Jesus freaks!

Today, in the spirit of both Whitehead and Jesus, I believe that God comes to us each moment of the day. I am not waiting for the constantly revised Second Coming in which an absentee God supernaturally intervenes to save "his" chosen ones, while leaving the Earth and its remaining inhabitants, our human and non-human kin, to the agony of hellfire and brimstone, as prelude to an earthly paradise for those who have the right theological formulae. That God is too small and distant, and ironically, despite the fundamentalist claims of divine intimacy, seems too abstract and inflexible, privileging cookie cutter doctrines over open-spirited and growing relationships. I believe in a Millisecond Coming, in which God is always with us, subtly guiding us and all creation in non-coercive ways. Each moment is revelatory, and each person bears something of God's wisdom and love, regardless of how hidden it may be to them or to me. God invites all of us to abundant life and all those invitations are personal and contextual. All of us are embraced by Divine Love and inscribed on the palms of God's hand. Amid the universality of revelation, there are special moments in which God of the Universe comes alive in our unique personal experiences and the Word becomes flesh in head, heart, and hands in our distinctive histories. These are the moments of conversion, religious ecstasy, moral and spiritual transformation, and mysticism, the "thin places," as Celtic Christians say, in which we experience the intimate dance of divinity and humanity in our lives and the world. The ordinary becomes extraordinary and the doors of perception are cleansed so that we experience the finite infinity of life, as American poet Emily Dickinson avers.

My first dramatic encounter with God – my first conversion experience in the lingo of evangelical Christianity - came at Leonard Eiler's Roundup for God, a dateable conversion experience in my ninth year. The second, though less dramatic, conversion experience came in mid-October 1970, when I received my mantra (a Sanskrit prayer word repeated as a way of focusing on the Divine) at the Students International Meditation Society in Berkeley, California. Following my initiation into Transcendental Meditation, I chose to quit drugs, alcohol, and meat, made meditation a daily practice for over fifty-five years, in particular the integration of TM, Healing Prayer, Scriptural Affirmations, and Centering Prayer. (I have since relaxed my abstinence in two of the three and ponder from a distance the growing interest in psilocybin as a tool for spiritual transformation.) Then, two weeks after learning Transcendental Meditation, I returned to Grace Baptist Church, a progressive American Baptist Church, a block from San Jose State Universities. The pastors John Akers and Shorty Collins saw a theologian and pastor in me and midwifed the first tentative steps which have led to nearly five decades of teaching and ministry. I am ever grateful to these "good ancestors," who still inspire me to join the Way of Jesus with social action and love for all God's children.

God is never done with us. God quietly guided my footsteps to Marie Fox's class on Plato's *Phaedrus* and later to enrolling in her course on Plato's *Timaeus*. I experienced the Platonic eros of intellectual mysticism and began my journey as a philosopher. A year later my pastor John Akers encouraged me to enroll in a class on Whitehead's Philosophy and its Religious Relevance, taught by Richard Keady, a recently minted Ph.D. student of John Cobb at Claremont, and former Roman Catholic priest, and I've never looked back, and have only grown in my faith, theological vision, and experience of God.

In reading Whitehead's and Plato's cosmological and theological writings, I found a philosophy and theology that gave shape to my growing experience as a young Christian. In joining my study of Whitehead and Plato, I discovered a world view and mystical vision – a third understated conversion experience – that has shaped my life ever since. I discovered a personal God I could believe in, who inspired a faith that joined East and West, embraced the mysticism of the Magical Mystery Tours of my counterculture adventures, con-templation and action, and enabled me to begin to experience Jesus once more as a personal companion. I discovered that Christian faith is a holy adventure, not stuck in the past but leaning toward new creation. My relationship with Jesus was rekindled: the Jesus I rediscovered was the lively and innovative embodiment of mysticism, healing, and prophetic protest. I found Jesus in my growing commitment to contemplative activism, in protesting the war in Vietnam and supporting Cesar Chavez and Dolores Huerta in their quest for justice for California's farmworkers.[5]

My footsteps were led to Claremont where I studied process theology with John Cobb, David Griffin, and Bernard Loomer, alongside my fellow theological companions Jay McDaniel, Catherine Keller, Ignacio Castuera, Rebecca Parker, and Rita Nakashima Brock. I continued my Platonic adventures in studying with Fred Sontag, the legendary Pomona College professor, and Claremont Graduate School professor Chuck Young, and eventually completed a dissertation in 1979 on the theme "Is Whitehead A Platonist? Creation and Causation in Plato's *Timaeus* and Whitehead's Cosmology?"

In reflecting on my over five-decade journey with Whitehead and Jesus, I recognize that this text is not the culmination of my adventures as a process theologian, Christian minister, and practicing Christian but an intimate and novel theological trajectory of seeing both Jesus and Whitehead in a new light and open to fresh future visions of divinity. My goal in this text is not scholastic exegesis of Whiteheadian cosmology, although I seek to be true both to the insights of Whitehead's philosophy and the Gospel vision of Jesus. Rather, my intent is to explore imaginatively as well as textually the impact of Jesus on Whitehead's philosophical vision, highlight the importance of Jesus for Christian process theologians, and inspire Christians to explore ways in which process theology can be enriched by a personal and mystical relationship with Jesus. I also believe that our understanding of Jesus can be enriched by the wisdom of Whitehead's vision. Although I travel beyond the boundaries of Whitehead's

---

5   For a discussion of contemplative activism, see my book, *Jesus: Mystic, Healer, and Prophet* (Vestal, NY: Anamchara Books, 2024).

written words, and go further than many Whitehead scholars might think warranted by the texts I cite, I am not baptizing Whitehead as an evangelical or church going Christian, but rather describing what I believe to be the impact of Jesus in Whitehead's vision of God and the world and the resources of a creative synthesis of Whitehead and Jesus for a vital, robust, spiritually alive and open Christian faith of the future. Raised in a profoundly religious home, the impact of his childhood faith in a Loving God enabled Whitehead to make sense of tragedy and formulate a metaphysical vision in which God is not an add on, but at the heart of the Cosmic Adventure.

My goal in describing the impact of Jesus in Whitehead's world view is to encourage inspiration and affirmation, and not conversion in the narrow sense of the word. Like my teacher John Cobb, I want to embrace, teach, and preach a lively, holistic, creatively transforming vision of Jesus, which joins contemplation and action and inspires followers and kin of Jesus to be God's companions in healing the earth. I seek a "bigger Jesus," known by love and hospitality, not exclusionary doctrines and spiritual exceptionalism.

John Cobb once stated that Christ is the way that excludes no way, and that is my affirmation, too: faithfulness to Jesus, especially the open-spirited Jesus of Whitehead's philosophy and process theology, opens us to appreciate truth wherever it is found, whether in the laboratory, archeological dig, classroom, the picket line, a child's drawing, or Zen Buddhist monastery. You can be a mystically and evangelically oriented follower of Jesus, influenced by American Transcendentalism, Hindu spirituality, and Taoist naturalism, as I am. You can also be a theologian whose faith is shaped by the Buddhist or African Yoruba traditions, like my colleagues Jay McDaniel and Monica Coleman. A process vision of Jesus and a Whiteheadian philosophy seen through the eyes of Jesus opens us to experiences of radical amazement, as Abraham Joshua Heschel says, and to greater depths and wider horizons of the faith Jesus affirmed and the God Jesus embodied. Jesus is historically and intimately localized in scripture and personal experience. Jesus is also universalized, unbounded, and global in impact, ranging far beyond the words of scripture or the Christian movement he inspired.

In this short text, I will share what I believe to be the impact of the life of Jesus in Whitehead's vision of God and the dynamic and interdependent nature of process-relational thought. I also will share how Whitehead's thought illumines the Gospel portraits of Jesus, enabling persons to join intimacy with universality in an ever-expanding circle of revelation and love. If Jesus is, indeed, the Word and Wisdom, Logos and Sophia, made flesh, as the Gospel of John proclaims, then Jesus is a window not only into God's heart but the dynamic, relational world in which we live. I believe that Christ can be good news for all people, breaking down all the walls of oppression, exclusion, and diminishment, as John Cobb asserts. I also believe that process-relational and open and relational theologies can "preach" in ways that transform our lives and personal and political values. The times call for passionate, open, mystical, earth-affirming, and progressive theological visions and interplay of Whiteheadian and process and relational theology and Jesus can feed the fire of faith in a pluralistic age.

This is a work of faith and love: love for Jesus and for the fallible yet inspirational and inclusive and evolving church that needs to claim its role as God's companion in healing the Earth. This is also a work of gratitude – "for all that has been - thanks," as Dag Hammarskjold says - to my teachers John Cobb, David Griffin, Bernard Loomer, Richard Keady, and Marie Fox and pastors who have shaped my theological and professional life, John Akers and George L. "Shorty" Collins as well as my first spiritual mentor my father Everett Epperly and my praying mother Loretta Epperly. My understanding of Whitehead and process theology has been enriched by nearly fifty years of theological and personal friendship with Jay McDaniel and Catherine Keller and my interactions with younger theologians whose work I've met along the way such as Thomas Jay Oord and my students in process theology. *Ubuntu,* "I am because of you. We are because of one another." As Hammarskjold continues, "for all that shall be – yes!" in its inspiration of the Great Yes of this text: the Yes of a lively, open, experiential, and healing faith for "just such a time as this."

JUST A CLOSER WALK WITH JESUS

Augustine of Hippo once counseled *Solvitur ambulando,* "it will be solved by walking." Faith is often described in terms of a pilgrimage and walking, whether on the highways and byways of Assisi with Francis, following the "way of the pilgrim in Russia," or sojourning on the Camino de Santiago. Healthy faith is on the move and growing. In my theospiritual orientation, the belief that theology and spirituality are companions and that from mystical experiences emerge theological concepts and the call to world transformation, each chapter concludes with a spiritual practice, reflective of Whitehead's vision of Jesus and Jesus' impact on Whitehead.

In this first practice, simply take a walk either on foot or in your imagination. As you walk, invite Jesus to walk with you. Visualize Jesus as an intimate companion, present beside you. (Jesus is present anyway, even if you are unaware of his presence!) As you walk along, share any thoughts, questions, or challenges with Jesus. As you share your deepest concerns with Jesus, take time to listen to any responses that emerge. Take time in the days ahead to see Jesus as your companion in the events of your life and call upon our Great Ancestor to guide, protect, encourage, and empower you.

Prayer for the Journey. In the words of the spiritual, "I Want Jesus to Walk with Me," I want you, O Jesus, to walk with me today and every day. All along my pilgrim journey, I want you, O Jesus, to walk with me. In my trials, please walk with me. When my heart is almost broken, please walk with me. When I'm in trouble, please walk with me. When I'm bowed down in sorrow, please walk with me. Loving Companion, walk with me and guide my steps on this pilgrim journey, open the path toward the future, and remind me that you are always with me to comfort, challenge, and care. In Jesus' Name. Amen.

CHAPTER TWO
WHITEHEAD'S REFLECTIONS
ON JESUS

> *Now after John was arrested, Jesus came to Galilee proclaim-*
> *ing the good news of God and saying, "The time is fulfilled, and*
> *the kingdom of God has come near; repent, and believe in the good*
> *news."* (John 1:14)

> *The power of God is the worship God inspires…The worship of*
> *God is not a rule of safety—it is an adventure of the spirit, a flight*
> *after the unattainable. The death of religion comes with the repression*
> *of the high hope of adventure.*[6]

Just as I was steeped in American evangelical Christianity reflected
in the faith of my pastor-father and the Baptist church, young Alfred
North Whitehead's spiritual roots were nourished by the intellectual and urbane Anglican tradition embodied by his pastor parent
and grandparent. Born in Ramsgate, England, in 1861, the son
of an Anglican minister and school master of the Chatham House
Academy, established by Whitehead's grandfather, Whitehead was
well-acquainted with the grand doctrinal, theological, and liturgical
traditions of Christianity. No doubt religious themes characterized
mealtime discussions. Like myself, I suspect the young Whitehead
went on pastoral calls with his father and grandfather, and regularly
encountered religious dignitaries at their parish church and in his
parents' parlor. In the best spirit of Anglican Christianity, I imagine
Whitehead memorizing the Apostles and Nicene Creeds, attending
church school and confirmation classes, and learning the heart of

---

6   Alfred North Whitehead, *Science and the Modern World* (New York: Free
Press, 1967), 192.

Christianity through liturgy and sermon. It is likely Whitehead heard hundreds of sermons, detailing the life and teachings of Jesus, not to mention singing carols and hymns celebrating Jesus' birth, death, and resurrection, as well as the life and ministry of Jesus. There is no indication that Whitehead enjoyed the emotional Christianity of my youth, nor was it likely that his cosmopolitan Anglican parish sponsored revival meetings like Leonard Eilers' "Roundup for God," but it is clear from his biographers, and his personal autobiographical sketch that he rejoiced in the countryside of his birthplace and reveled in times of solitude and study.[7] He was, like the young evangelical child born 91 years after Whitehead's birth, to the Christian manor born, and was directly and indirectly shaped by religious imagery and doctrine throughout his life despite (or because) of his interest in mathematics and science.

On more than one occasion, Whitehead affirmed that philosophy begins with wonder. As a child, the future philosopher was a "quick learner," who had "a great deal of free time. Much of it was spent outdoors…He had more time than a schoolboy would have had for solitary wondering about everything he saw." Later in life, Whitehead asserted that "he was no good unless he had a couple hours each day in which he could go off by himself and think."[8] Whitehead noted that authentic religion involves solitude as well as society. Although there is no documentary evidence, based on Whitehead's own words and my understanding of philosophy in the Platonic tradition that shaped both Whitehead and myself, philosophical reflection is seen as a spiritual practice not unlike meditation.

As a student at Cambridge, Whitehead's spirit and intellect expanded because of relationships he cultivated in his participation in the school's elite conversation society, "The Apostles." In the Society's dialogues, Whitehead responded to the question, "Shall we transcend

7   Paul Arthur Schilpp, editor, *Whitehead: Library of Living Philosophers,* volume 3, (Evanston,IL: Northwestern University Press, 1941).
8   Victor Lowe, *Whitehead: The Man and His W*ork (Baltimore: Johns Hopkins Press, 1985), 32-33.

our limitations?" with a mystical aspiration, "I want to see God." We do not know whether his prayer was answered through mystical vision or philosophical speculation. However, the quest for a dynamic and lively vision of God was at the heart of Whitehead's North American philosophical visions. Whitehead believed that deep down cosmology had a mystical element in its quest to describe the ultimate horizons of our lives. According to the mature Whitehead:

> The use of philosophy is to maintain an active novelty of fundamental ideas illuminating the social system…If you like to phrase it so, philosophy is mystical. For mysticism is insight into the depths as yet unspoken. But the purpose of philosophy is to rationalize mysticism: not by explaining it away, but by the introduction of novel verbal characterizations, rationally coordinated.
>
> Philosophy is akin to poetry, and both of them attempt to express that ultimate good sense that we call civilization. In each case there is a reference to form beyond the direct meaning of words.[9]

For a period of eight years during his tenure as a professor at Cambridge, Whitehead took a great interest in theology. He even briefly considered converting to Roman Catholicism. Biographer Lucien Price notes that Whitehead's religious explorations were:

> all extracurricular, but so thorough that he amassed a sizable theological library. He dismissed the subject and sold the books. A Cambridge bookseller was willing to give quite a handsome figure for the collection. It then appeared that the pay must be taken in books at his shop. So he went on an orgy of book-buying until he had overdrawn his account.[10]

---

9   Alfred North Whitehead, *Modes of Thought* (New York: Free Press, 1968), 174.ener
10   Lucien Price, *Dialogues with Alfred North Whitehead* (Boston: Little, Brown and Company, 1954), 9.

The reality of death often compels us to return to the eternal verities of life. In a world of perpetual perishing processes, we need a solid rock upon which to stand. Even if the energetic occasions comprising the rock are constantly changing, our emotional and spiritual well-being requires a dependable reality that endures through all life's changes. In his later philosophical work, Whitehead cited the words of the grand Anglican hymn, penned by Scottish cleric Henry Francis Lyte, "Abide with me," as an example of the dynamic interplay of flux and permanence and novelty and order, both of which are revelations of the divine, the rock on which we stand and the most moved mover. This is true for me in my early seventies and for Whitehead in late sixties as we ponder the interplay of time and eternity: "Abide with me, fast falls the eventide."[11]

In his early fifties, there were signs that Whitehead was reclaiming his prior interest in philosophy and religion. In 1911, Whitehead began a twelve-year stint holding professorial and administrative posts at the University of London, where he took the first steps in returning to his previous interest in philosophical and theological reflection. We can suspect that his philosophical questions became more existentially important during the carnage of World War I, the war to end all wars! The death of his aviator son Eric, as well as the death and disability of a generation of young men, many of whom were his students and younger colleagues, may have inspired the mathematician to seek the consolations of metaphysics and religion, and may have inspired Whitehead's vision of an intimate and relational God, "the fellow sufferer who understands."[12]

Cosmology is personal as well as cosmic. Jesus lived in an oppressed land in which violence was a daily reality. Whitehead experienced similar violence in the slaughter of the innocents on the fields of war. The presence of God in the world, both as the source of possibility and preservation of value, the primordial and consequent natures of

---

11   Henry Francis Lyte, "Abide with Me."
12   Alfred North Whitehead, *Process and Reality: Corrected Edition.* (New York: Free Press, 1978),351.

God respectively, enabled Whitehead to imagine a world in which nothing is ever lost, and the ambiguities of life find healing in the experience of God's and our experiences of "tragic beauty." In God's experience, our lives perish and yet live evermore.[13]

Still, while some embrace dogmatic certainty in response to the realities of change and death, Whitehead saw the quest for truth, indeed, the quest for God as a holy adventure. I suspect that many readers were surprised at Whitehead's meditations on religion in the final pages of *Science and the Modern World*. Religion and science are not foes, but share an open-spirited quest for truth, motivated by a "high hope for adventure." At their best, science and religion are experimental and embrace change even if it means challenging previous understandings of reality and divinity. Dogmatism stifles both science and religion.

> I have been fooled once and I'll be damned if I'll be fooled again! Einstein is supposed to have made an epochal discovery [demolishing Newtonian certainty]. I am respectful and interested but also skeptical. There is no more reason to expect that Einstein's relativity is anything final, than Newton's *Principia*. The danger is dogmatic thought; it plays the devil with religion; and science is not immune from it.[14]

Our most cherished world views, scientific knowledge, and religious beliefs need to be constantly open to creative transformation as we encounter new experiences. Whitehead believed that there can never be dogmatic finality in our religious and scientific adventures. Always leave the windows of your mind open for new inspirations from God's Adventurous Spirit.

Whitehead believed that religion was an adventure of the spirit, which sometimes inspired geographical peregrinations, and in his sixties, Whitehead and his wife Evelyn embarked on holy adventure

---

13   Ibid., 351.
14   Lucien Price, Dialogues with Alfred North Whitehead (New York: Little Brown and Company, 1954), 345-346.

to the United States. In 1924, at age sixty-three, Whitehead was invited to join the faculty of Harvard University, where he taught in the philosophy department until 1937. At Harvard, Whitehead was free to speculate on metaphysics, intellectual history, and religious experience. Whitehead's American adventure inspired the aging philosopher to dialogue with his youthful faith in new and creative ways. Although Whitehead never aligned himself with a Christian congregation in Cambridge, Massachusetts, he reclaimed his interest in Jesus, and came to believe Jesus, along with Plato, was the most important figure in the shaping of Western civilization. Whitehead's Jesus, as we will see, reflects the highest values of human existence and reveals the cosmic movements reflected in God's aim at the production of beauty.

Whitehead's Jesus is not locked in the past but invites to articulate in the present and future new visions of God, human existence, ethics, and spirituality. Equally true for religion as well as science and philosophy, "the vitality of thought is an adventure. That is what I have been saying all my life, and I have said little else. Ideas won't keep. Something must be done about them...the meaning of life is adventure."[15]

A Philosopher Speaks of Jesus. Whitehead did not presume to be a Bible scholar, but he was raised in home where the Bible and the Book of Common Prayer shaped his family's life and education. He grew up listening to scripture and singing hymns in church. Like another youth growing up in 1950s California, he wanted to "see God." I imagine that he heard the stories of Jesus and understood the flow of time in terms of the cycle of Christian holidays -Christmas, Good Friday, and Easter – and the seasons of the Christian year from Advent to Pentecost. Even when he no longer regularly attended church, the life and teachings of Jesus were in his bones and, as I believe, essential, along with twenty-first century science and the history of philosophy, in shaping his world view. In this section, we will reflect on Whitehead's explicit comments on the life of Jesus as a portal to

15   Lucien Price, *Dialogues of Alfred North Whitehead,* 254.

understanding the impact of Jesus on his spiritual, ethical, and meta-physical vision. Although Whitehead cited Jesus explicitly in only a handful of passages in *Science and the Modern World* (1925), *Religion in the Making* (1926), *Process and Reality* (1929), and *Adventures in Ideas* (1933), I believe these texts illuminate Whitehead's philosophical system, especially his understanding of the relational and expansive nature of God and the shape of God's relationship to humankind and the world as dynamic, relational, persuasive, and compassionate.

Whitehead's first significant comments on Jesus occur in *Religion in the Making*, a text which reflects the philosopher's unique vision of God that gave birth to the metaphysical reflections of *Process and Reality* and inspired the emergence of process theology.

Although he recognized that doctrine could easily lead to dogmatism, Whitehead affirmed the importance of doctrine in the evolution of religious experience. In speaking of the origins of Buddhism and Christianity, Whitehead notes:

> Buddhism and Christianity find their origins respectively in two inspired moments of history: the life of Buddha, and the life of Christ. Buddha gave his doctrine to enlighten the world; Christ gave his life. It is for Christians to discern the doctrine.[16]

Christianity is a religion in the making. Incarnational and embodied and mystical rather than philosophical and intellectual in origins, it finds its inspiration in the life of Jesus, and the simplicity of the Galilean teacher, who challenged religious authorities with his vision of God's all-embracing love. God's realm is not abstract and distant; it is among us in flesh and blood and the experiences of transformed lives. In contrast to spiritual demagogues and the authoritarian and violent gods they privilege, "the life of Christ is not an expedition of over-ruling power…Its power lies in the absence of force. It has the decisiveness of a supreme ideal, and that is why the history of the world divides at this point in time."[17]

16   Whitehead, *Religion in the Making* , 55.
17   Alfred North Whitehead, *Adventures in Ideas* (New York: Free Press, 1033), 56-57.

In the Galilean origins of Christianity, we discern a quantum leap in our understandings of God and ourselves. Fear-based, backward-looking religion, gives way to the forward movements of the Spirit in history, inviting us to seek to become as much like God in character as possible. Perhaps Whitehead, the mature philosopher, remembered singing the "Once in Royal David's City" as he penned the words of *Religion in the Making*.

> For he is our childhood's pattern;
> Day by day like us he grew,
> He was little, weak, and helpless,
> Tears and smiles like us he knew:
> And he feeleth for our sadness,
> And he shareth in our gladness.[18]

In looking to the life of Jesus, we see God's nature and discover the highest possibilities for our own lives. Liberated from fear, we can live boldly embodying God's vision in transforming our world. We can immerse ourselves in healing relationships and claim our vocation as God's companions in promoting the well-being of all creation. While Jesus is not explicitly mentioned in the following passage, the imagery of divine companionship reflects what it means to see Jesus as model and companion in the joys and sorrows, triumphs and struggles of life.

> The new, and almost profane, concept of the goodness of God replaces the older emphasis on the will of God. In communal religion you study the will of God in order that he may preserve you; in a purified religion, rationalized under the influence of the world-concept, you study his goodness in order to be like him. It is the difference between the enemy you conciliate and the companion whom you imitate…If the modern world is to find God, it must find him through love and not through fear, with the help of John and not of Paul."[19]

---

18   Cecil Frances Alexander, "Once in Royal David's City,"
19   Alfred North Whitehead, *Religion in the Making* (New York: Meridian,

Jesus is the incarnation of Divine Goodness and the model for Christian living. The life of Jesus in its concreteness is both intimate and infinite, historical and global, rooted in time and yet transcending his social location, and like that of Gautama, Moses, Mohammed, and Isaiah, forms not only our personal and social ethics but our vision of reality. Mysticism illuminates everyday life and inspires us to become part of the mission of moving from self-interest to world loyalty.

> Religion bases itself primarily upon a small selection of the common experiences of the race…religion claims that its concepts, though derived primarily from special experiences, are yet of universal validity to be applied by faith to the ordering of all experience.
>
> Rational religion appeals to the direct intuition of special occasions, and to the elucidatory power of its concepts for all occasions. It arises from that which is special, but extends to what is general.[20]

In recognizing the interplay of solitude, sacrifice, and society, our vision of Jesus and other great religious leaders provides inspiration, aspiration, and illumination for charting our daily lives and quest for "the more perfect union" in politics, economics, and jurisprudence.

> The great religious conceptions which haunt the imaginations of mankind are scenes of solitariness. Prometheus chained to his rock, Mahomet brooding in the desert, the meditations of the Buddha, the solitary Man on the cross."[21]

For Whitehead, the life of Jesus along with the Plato's vision of creation as the victory of persuasion over force transforms the trajectory of Western civilization. The highest values in religion, politics, and personal relationships are found in Plato's affirmation that "the divine element in the world is to be perceived as a persuasive agency and not

1960), 40,73.
20   Ibid., 31.
21   Alfred North Whitehead, *Religion in the Making* , 19.

as a coercive agency," which should be seen as "one of the greatest intellectual discoveries in the history of religion." Whitehead adds that "the second phase is the supreme moment in religious history, according to Christianity. The essence of Christianity was the appeal to the life of Christ and his agency in the world."[22]

Although he was no doubt aware of the various scholarly quests for the historical Jesus, Whitehead does not attempt a scholarly analysis of Jesus' life. The impact of Jesus is to be found in his person and way of life and not in Christological doctrines, which often transform the living and loving Jesus into an abstract figure to whom we must declare our loyalty or face divine punishment. In language bordering on poetry that inspires metaphysics as well as politics, Whitehead rhapsodizes:

> But there can be no doubt as to what elements in the [gospel] record have evoked a response from all that is best in human nature. The Mother, the Child, the bare manger: the lowly man, homeless and self-forgetful, with his message of peace, love, and sympathy: the suffering, the agony, the tender words as life ebbed, the final despair: the whole with the authority of supreme victory. I need not elaborate. Can there be any doubt that the power of Christianity lies in its revelation in act, of that which Plato divined in theory?[23]

Whitehead's philosophical vision of the universality of divine revelation found in the moment-by-moment impact of the initial aim, or divine possibility, in each occasion of experience as well as the global divine aim at beauty, enables the philosopher to affirm that Jesus not only reveals God's deepest nature, and is a source of cosmological reflection, but that Jesus is also revelatory of God's universal creative wisdom revealed in the philosophy of Plato.

Whitehead sees Jesus as the reflection of God's presence in the world. God is the Beyond Within. The Infinite energizing and guiding the finite. The Cosmic God is our Loving Companion. Loving

---
22   Whitehead, *Adventures in ideas,* 166-167.
23   Ibid., 167.

interdependence characterizes humankind at its best and is found throughout the universe. Whitehead notes two ways Jesus transformed the Hebraic vision of God:

> The association of God with the Kingdom of Heaven, coupled with the explanation that "The Kingdom of Heaven is within you." The second point is the concept of God under the metaphor of father… "God is love."[24]

Divine transcendence is qualified and transformed by God's immanence in our lives and the world. God is truly with us, in us, and among us. As Whitehead further notes, "God is [an immanent] factor in the universe…We find in these Logia of Christ the saying, 'Cleave the wood and I am there.'" This is merely one example of an emphatic assertion of immanence.[25]

The immanent and ever-present God is our constant companion, the fellow sufferer who understands, and the Jesus who "walks with us and talks with us and tells us we are his own" in loving intimacy and wise guidance.

Process theologian and biblical scholar Terrence Fretheim notes that it is more important to ask the question, "What kind of God do you believe in?" than "Do you believe in God?" Our deepest held beliefs shape our character. Relational images of God lead to universalist understandings of revelation and the affirmation of agency and diversity. Authoritarian images of God lead to heresy hunting, ostracism of those who differ from us, and passivity before the Almighty. They also lead to the followers of the authoritarian God forcefully embodying a "manifest destiny" as God's chosen ones in bringing their vision of God's will to the world by dominating and destroying those whom they perceive as unbelievers or lesser humans.

> When the Western world accepted Christianity, Caesar conquered…The brief Galilean vision of humility flickered

---

24   *Religion in the Making*, 70.
25   Ibid., 71,

throughout the ages, uncertainly. In the official formation of the religion, it has assumed the trivial form of the mere attribution of to the Jews that they cherished a misconception about their Messiah. But the deeper idolatry, of the fashioning of God in the image of the Egyptian, Persian, and Roman imperial rulers was retained. The Church gave unto God the attributes which belonged exclusively to Caesar.[26]

To secure its dominance over Western civilization, Christian leaders traded the intimate and relational love of a personal and empathetic God for the unilateral and coercive power of a distant and demanding God. Many still do! Fueled by the quest for power and compelled by dogmatic certainty, the persecuted became the persecutors and the open-spirited faith of Jesus was reduced to closed minded dogma. The ecclesiastical and political followers of Jesus restricted the "keys to the kingdom" to loyal and obedient subjects, fearful of retaliation in this life and the next, and condemned theological, racial, and spiritual outsiders to the outer darkness of eternal damnation. To followers of the authoritarian and coercive God, revelation and salvation belong to those who possessed ecclesiastical, scriptural, and sacramental authority, reflected in a narrow understanding of divine revelation and compassion. Innovation and questioning are seen as threats to divine sovereignty and often were met with inquisition, persecution, and intellectual martyrdom. The living and embodied Jesus is transformed into an abstract doctrine to be believed rather than a companion and guide to cherish and incarnate in the concrete encounters of daily life and citizenship. Although not restricted to Christianity, authoritarian images of God transformed the persecuted church and its crucified savior into agents of persecution and intellectual, political, and personal violence, as we tragically see in the Crusades, the scriptural justification of slavery, theories of a master race among the Nazis, and today's white Christian nationalism and backward-looking and exclusivist politics.

26   Alfred North *Whitehead, Process and Reality*, 345.

The intellectually dense language of Whitehead's metaphysics reveals a vision of God in stark contrast to the authoritarian, domineering, all-determining, and punitive God prized by many Christians and enforced on religious non-conformists and ethnic "others." God is love and we find the God of Jesus in loving relationships to all humankind and the non-human world.

> The action of the fourth phase [the superjective nature of God] is the love of God for the world. It is the particular providence for particular occasions. What is done in the world is transformed into a reality in heaven, and the reality in heaven passes back into the world. By reason of this reciprocal relation, the love in the world passes into the love in heaven and floods back into the world. In this sense, God is the great companion – the fellow sufferer who understands.[27]

A God-filled world reflects the dynamic, innovative, interdependence seen in the life of Jesus. In many ways, Whitehead's cosmology of compassion reflects, even in a world characterized by contrast and conflict, the priority of relationship over individualism and empathy over apathy found incarnate in Jesus.

JUST A CLOSER WALK WITH JESUS

For centuries, followers of Jesus have taken comfort in the Jesus Prayer, "Lord Jesus Christ, have mercy upon me, a sinner." The prayer has its origins in the parable of the publican, religious leader, and the sinner, found in Luke 18:9-14.

> To some who were confident of their own righteousness and looked down on everyone else, Jesus told this parable: "Two men went up to the temple to pray, one a Pharisee and the other a tax collector. The Pharisee stood by himself and prayed: "God, I thank you that I am not like other people—robbers, evildoers,

---

27   Ibid., 351.

adulterers—or even like this tax collector. I fast twice a week and give a tenth of all I get."

"But the tax collector stood at a distance. He would not even look up to heaven, but beat his breast and said, 'God, have mercy on me, a sinner.' "I tell you that this man, rather than the other, went home justified before God. For all those who exalt themselves will be humbled, and those who humble themselves will be exalted."

While this prayer recognizes our imperfection and finitude and need for God's grace, I believe its deeper meaning is relational in its portrayal of the graceful interdependence of life, revealed in the character of God's creative-responsive love, which protects, sustains, transforms, and enables us to begin after personal failure, whether that failure involves pain we have caused, the loss of professional status, alienation from another. As a child I sang the hymn, "I Need Thee Every Hour," not fully knowing the meaning of the words.

I need Thee, oh, I need Thee;
Ev'ry hour I need Thee;
Oh, bless me now, my Savior,
I come to Thee.[28]

Now in my seventh decade, I recognize my need for God's grace to make it through each day, to face my imperfections and fears, to be compassionate on those whom I love and those who I perceive as enemies, and to face what is out of my control in the aging process of body, mind, and spirit, and anticipatory and present experiences of grief and loss. The Jesus Prayer reminds me that God is loving and merciful and present to respond, in the context of my agency, to my every need. "Nothing can separate me from the love of God that is in Christ Jesus our Lord." (Romans 8:39)

The Russian spiritual classic *The Way of a Pilgrim* charts a simple man's walk with God. With every step, the pilgrim repeats the Jesus

---

28   Annie S. Hawks and Robert Lowry, "I Need Thee Every Hour."

Prayer, "Lord Jesus, Son of God, have mercy on me." The pilgrim advises, "as you draw your breath in, say, or imagine yourself saying, 'Lord Jesus Christ,' and as you breathe again, 'have mercy on me.'"

Take time to pray the Jesus Prayer while sitting or walking. Breathe deeply and fully. Inhaling as you say, "Lord, Jesus Christ," or "Jesus" and exhaling with the words, "Have mercy on me."

Prayer for the Journey. Loving Jesus, let me pray in the spirit of another spiritual: Guide my feet, while I run this race. Guide my thoughts while I run this race. Stand by me while I run this race. Search my heart while I run this race. Let me know that I am your child while I run this race for I don't want to run this race in vain. In Jesus' Name. Amen.29

---

29   African American spiritual, "Guide My Feet"

CHAPTER THREE
JESUS AND THE REALM OF GOD

May your kingdom come.
May your will be done
on earth as it is in heaven. (Matthew 6:10)

> *For the perfected actuality [present immortally in God's consequent nature] passes back into the temporal world, and qualifies this world so that each temporal actuality includes it as an immediate fact of relevant experience. For the kingdom of heaven is with us today. The action of the fourth phase [the superjective nature of God] is the love of God for the world. It is the particular providence for particular occasions. What is done in the world is transformed into a reality in heaven, and the reality in heaven passes back into the world. By reason of this reciprocal relation, the love in the world passes into the love in heaven and floods back into the world. In this sense, God is the great companion – the fellow sufferer who understands.[30]*

A cosmopolitan thinker, raised on the scriptures and liturgies of the church, Alfred North Whitehead recognized the importance of the realm, kindom, or kingdom of God, in Jesus' teaching. It is probable that Whitehead was familiar with the various lives of Jesus, penned by scholars in the nineteenth century, and may have dialogued with British colleagues about Albert Schweitzer's emphasis of the centrality of eschatology, or God's future realm, in Schweizer's epoch-making *Quest for the Historical Jesus – From Reimarus to Wrede*, first published in 1906.

---

30   Ibid., 351.

Whitehead began his Harvard adventures at the height of the American Social Gospel movement, inspired by its vision of the importance of human agency in realizing God's realm on Earth as it is embodied in the quest for economic justice, safe working conditions, fair wages, unionization, child welfare, and racial equality. In light of his own cosmopolitan spirituality and liberal politics, Whitehead's religious vision was this worldly in its quest for a civilization guided by the vision of truth, beauty, and goodness. Whitehead's hope was for the realization of the values of truth, beauty, and goodness in this world and in our personal and political experience and not in a disembodied heavenly realm. The universal aim at the production of beauty is ethical as well as metaphysical, social as well as personal, and long term as well as immediate.

Jesus and the Realm of God. Jesus was a child of the Hebraic prophets and the embodiment of the prophetic vision of Shalom, the realm of wholeness, justice, and reconciliation, was at the heart of his ministry. For the prophets, history was meaningful and purposive. God was alive and present as the Restless Spirit moving within history toward the realization of an age in which:

The wolf shall live with the lamb;
     the leopard shall lie down with the kid;
the calf and the lion will feed together,
     and a little child shall lead them.
The cow and the bear shall graze;
     their young shall lie down together;
     and the lion shall eat straw like the ox.
The nursing child shall play over the hole of the asp,
     and the weaned child shall put its hand on the adder's den.
They will not hurt or destroy
     on all my holy mountain,
for the earth will be full of the knowledge of the Lord
     as the waters cover the sea. (Isaiah 11:6-9)

The prophet Isaiah and the prophetic tradition Jesus embraced sought to incarnate, as Walter Brueggeman asserted, an alternative reality to our current state of injustice, violence, dehumanization, and environmental destruction.[31] In the prophets' dream, all people shall find a home in Jerusalem and friend and enemy shall be reconciled. The rich and the poor will join hands to bring about a new age in which every child has a home, good food, and hope for the future. The prophetic, reflected in the words of Amos, challenged the current order of life in light of God's vision of a time in which:

Justice will roll down like water
And righteousness like an ever-flowing stream.
(Amos 5:24)

I believe that Jesus was the incarnation of God's prophetic vision in a way that initiated a new global spiritual movement while honoring the wisdom of his Jewish parents then and now. Filled with the Spirit, Jesus' mother Mary of Nazareth proclaims a new world order in which the poor are uplifted while the wealthy give up their privilege:

God has shown strength with his arm;
  he has scattered the proud
  in the imagination of their hearts.
He has brought down the powerful from their thrones
  and lifted up the lowly;
  he has filled the hungry with good things
  and sent the rich away empty. (Luke 1:51-53)

Following the baptismal call of the Spirit affirming Jesus' vocation as God's Beloved Child, his spiritual retreat in wilderness, and the arrest of his spiritual companion John the Baptist, Jesus "came to Galilee, proclaiming the good news of God, and saying, 'The time is

---

31   For the prophetic tradition, see Bruce Epperly, *The Prophet Amos Speaks to America,* Walter Brueggemann, *The Prophetic Imagination* (Minneapolis: Fortress Press, 1978), and Abraham Joshua Heschel, *The Prophets* (Peabody, MA: Hendrickson Publishers, 1973).

fulfilled, and the kingdom of God has come near, repent, and believe in the good news.'" (Mark 1:14-15)

God's realm is among us, embodied in the growth of seeds to trees and the rising of bread. (Luke 17:20-21) Although God's realm may come dramatically, God is most present in the quiet movements of creative transformation in our lives and in the non-human world and natural world of flora and fauna. In each moment of life, God calls us to be light givers and salt, leaven and geminating seeds, moment by moment giving birth by our actions and citizenship to God's realm of Shalom, God's Peaceable Commonwealth, on earth. (Matthew 5:13-16) God's vision of Shalom emerges relationally and not coercively, inviting rather than demanding, inspiring rather than frightening, as it challenges us to be God's head, heart, and hands in healing the world.

Jesus' dream of a transformed world and a transformed humankind is grounded in interplay of divine possibility and human response. Quoting and claiming the prophet Isaiah's vision as his spiritual vocation, Jesus proclaims his mission statement:

> The Spirit of the Lord is upon me,
>   because he has anointed me
>   to bring good news to the poor.
> He has sent me to proclaim release to the captives
>   and recovery of sight to the blind,
>   to set free those who are oppressed,
> to proclaim the year of the Lord's favor. (Luke 4:18-19)

Jesus' hometown listeners were astounded by his words and proud of the local prophet until the youthful prophet asserted that God's realm embraces the foreigner and those from whom we are estranged. In a blink of an eye, they moved from appreciation to anger when Jesus asserted that the realm of God is universal, touching friend and enemy, oppressed and oppressor, companion and stranger, and breaking down all the barriers in human relationships and the relationship of humankind to nature.

Jesus was a loyal son of Israel who also saw God's vision moving through all things to reconcile creation in all its diversity. The sun shines and the rain falls on the righteous and unrighteous, the clean and unclean alike. Our enemies and the undesirables in our midst – the Samaritan, Gentile, tax collector, the person with ritually unclean diseases, and prostitute – are as beloved by God as we are. The moral and spiritual arcs of history, to expand on Unitarian pastor and abolitionist Theodore Parker's vision, are constantly moving forward in concert with human agency toward the "more perfect union" in our civil life and global citizenship. God's love centers on each of us and embraces all of us.

Jesus' mission is to bring abundant life to our planet joining the healing of persons and communities. (John 10:10) God calls, but we must respond. We must repent, turn around, align ourselves with God's vision, and embody God's realm in daily life, citizenship, economics, and politics. We must follow in Jesus' footsteps, living as if God's realm is alive in our world and shaping our personal and political decisions long before it comes to pass. While Jesus, as a citizen of an occupied land without political power, primarily focused on the spirituality and ethics of individuals and small groups of followers, Jesus was clear that there was only "one world," that God's realm touches every aspect of life and that even the politically powerless must dream of a world in which the nations recognize God in "the least of these." (Matthew 25:31-46)

In a time of persecution and occupation – and Jesus and his first followers never experienced a moment of political freedom or the power to effect political change – we are challenged to pray with Jesus for a new world order and then put our prayers into action in the spirit of Abraham Joshua Heschel who proclaimed that his legs were praying as he marched with Martin Luther King. Jesus taught his followers to pray:

May your kingdom come.
May your will be done
    on earth as it is in heaven. (Matthew 6:10)

Challenging all forms of world denial and unworldly spirituality, Jesus proclaimed the goal of God's realm is coming to pass "on earth," right where we are in the challenges of economics, family life, diversity, and political decision-making. In so doing, Jesus joined prayer and protest and contemplation and action. We are not bystanders in the quest for God's realm. We are not to wait passively for God's realm to come in some undefined and constantly updated future: we are actors in its realization in our world. We are, as Teresa of Avila asserts, God's hands and feet in the emergence of God's realm in the world. History is constantly motivated by God's dream of Shalom. We are the incarnation of Jesus' vision, who are called to do "greater things" in the global and personal incarnation of Jesus' mission. (John 14:12) Yet the realization of God's dream in its fullness will come about only as we claim our vocation as God's companions in healing the Earth. In the words of June Jordan's "Poem for the South African Women," right now in this time and place, "we are the ones that we have been waiting for."

For Jesus, the realm of God, God's kingdom, moves through our lives and history. Like the mustard seed, it quietly provides moment by moment inspiration and wisdom. God has a dream, shares that dream with us, provides the erotic energy to motivate our quest, and invites us to live by the vision of Wholeness. History matters and our actions matter to our families, neighbors, nation, planet, and they matter to God. We can be part of a great adventure when we open to and align ourselves with God's moral and spiritual arc moving through our lives and the world.

Whitehead and the Realm of God. For Whitehead, the realm of God reflects God's vision embodied in possibilities relevant to each moment of experience, reflective of God's vision for the long haul of planetary and universal history. While Whitehead's term "initial aim" is rather dry and scholastic, the vision of divine possibility, local and global, spiritual and secular, suggested by God's moment by moment vision is breathtaking. Each moment emerges from our experience of the Divine Eros to actualize beauty, complexity, and intensity of experience for ourselves and for the world around us. The currents of divine possibility, like the moral arc of justice, flow in and through us, as reflections of the teleology of the universe as it aims toward beauty locally and globally, momentarily and over our lifespan. In the contours of God's presence in the world, Whitehead asserts that:

> [God's] purpose is always embodied in the particular ideals relevant to the actual state of the world. Thus all attainment is immortal in that it fashions the actual ideas which are God in the world as it is now. Every act leaves the world with a deeper or fainter impress of God. He then passes into his next relation to the world with enlarged, or diminished, presentation of ideal values.[32]

Whitehead's God is active in history without being coercive. As we will see in the next chapter, God's quest for Shalom and Beauty is grounded in the call and response of divine possibility and human agency: God's action is always intimate, contextual, and historical. The shape of divine activity is intimately related to the world that shapes God's experience. The realm of God is truly in us and with us as the energy of love, bestowing upon each moment of experience, a possibility or an array of possibilities, aimed at our wholeness and the wholeness of the world around us. What we do matters to God and can forward or delay God's vision of truth, beauty, goodness, and justice for ourselves and the world. The non-coercive relational God is incarnate in the world as it us, luring it toward what it can become.

The words with which this chapter began bear repeating. Can you imagine the reaction of Whitehead's first listeners and readers as they confronted a heart-felt and pietistic description of a personal God in the concluding section of Whitehead's cosmology and realized that

32   Whitehead, *Religion in the Making*, 152.

these apparently marginal words were at the heart of the philosopher's vision. Perhaps, some of the more religious readers even were inspired to think of Jesus' ministry as they pondered Whitehead's vision of God's presence in the world in terms of relational power, what John Cobb and Dave Griffin describe as "creative-responsive love."33

> For the perfected actuality [present immortally in God's consequent nature] passes back into the temporal world, and qualifies this world so that each temporal actuality includes it as an immediate fact of relevant experience. For the kingdom of heaven is with us today. The action of the fourth phase [the superjective nature of God] is the love of God for the world. It is the particular providence for particular occasions. What is done in the world is transformed into a reality in heaven, and the reality in heaven passes back into the world. By reason of this reciprocal relation, the love in the world passes into the love in heaven and floods back into the world. In this sense, God is the great companion – the fellow sufferer who understands.34

For the cosmologist Whitehead, the realm of God is God's love for the world, "the particular providence for particular occasions." This is not peripheral to Whitehead's metaphysics, but at the heart of his vision of the universe in which compassionate and evolutionary possibilities are joined with chance, necessity, recalcitrance, and agency. God's love is intimate, not abstract, contextual, not timeless, and historical, not ethereal. This is the love that Jesus embodied. Jesus treated each person as unique, calling forth the vision of what was possible for them in their current life situation. God wants us to have abundant life – intensity and complexity of experience – as we live out loud as God's light in the world. This is the nature of love: to be personal, intimate, and local, affirmative and inspirational. Jesus imagined creative futures within the realm of God for every person he encountered: the tax collector Zacchaeus, the rich young ruler,

33   John Cobb and David Ray Griffin
34   Whitehead, *Process and Reality*, 351.

the woman caught in adultery and her accusers, the woman with
the flow of blood, the comatose twelve-year-old girl, the vacillating
Peter, and the anxious Martha. In the Garden, Jesus calls the grief-
stricken Mary of Magdala by name, "Mary." In the words of today's
Black Lives Matter movement, Jesus said her name! "Mary!" and she
was transformed. While the good news of Jesus – and God's aim – is
global as well as local, we can each affirm the words of the hymn,
noted earlier in this book.

> And He walks with me, and He talks with me,
> And He tells me I am His own;
> And the joy we share as we tarry there,
> None other has ever known.[35]

In the intersection of cosmology and spirituality, God has a personal
relationship with every speck of creation and every person. God has a
personal relationship with you and me: evoking moment by moment
the dream of what we can become as citizens of God's realm of justice
and wholeness. God experiences our lives intimately and personally,
as we will discover in the next chapter, and God's experience of our
lives serves as the source of God's movements in our lives.

In the world envisioned by Jesus and Whitehead, God meets us
where we are, but God does not leave us there. Divine acceptance is
completed by Divine inspiration and challenge. During the course
of nearly six decades of theological travels from the summer of love,
discovering TM, encountering Whitehead and process theology, and
embracing Jesus as mystic, healer, and prophet, I heard a call and
response to the childhood hymn "Blessed assurance": to the words,
"blessed assurance, Jesus is mine," echoed, attributed to pastor-activist
William Sloan Coffin, "blessed disturber, I am his." The call of the
realm of God is toward future possibility and to the incarnation of
Shalom. The aim of God always takes us beyond ourselves to become
participants and partners in the realization of God's moral and spiritual
arc, in the global and long-term healing of the Earth. As Whitehead

35   Charles Miles, "In the Garden."

notes, once again in surprising words on the philosophy of science, that apply to the totality of our spiritual adventures.

> The worship of God is not a rule of safety—it is an adventure of the spirit, a flight after the unattainable. The death of religion comes with the repression of the high hope of adventure.[36]

God's realm is the invitation to live a holy adventure, whether you are in the supermarket shopping for guests, volunteering at the soup kitchen or in the aftermath of a climate-related disaster, picking up a child or grandchild at school, working at home or the office, or participating in our nation's politics. *Plus ultra*, "there is more," in God's Holy Adventure as God's realm meets us personally and contextually in every encounter, challenging us to do something beautiful for our neighbor, our community, and for the One to Whom All Hearts are Open and All Desires Known and All Possibilities Imagined.

JUST A CLOSER WALK WITH JESUS

The realm of God was at the heart of Jesus' vision of reality. God's presence in the world is guided by God's aim at Shalom and Wholeness for persons and community. God's presence touches each life. The Spirit that blessed Jesus at his baptism, giving him a sense of vocation, blesses each person moment by moment and over a lifespan in the context of God's long-term goals for history. God's call often comes "softly and tenderly." It may also come as the prophetic challenge to our lifestyle and politics.

Whitehead affirms that God provides a vision for each moment of experience. This intimate and global vision, described as God's initial aim, provides each creature with the highest possibilities for each moment of its life. God's aim is always personal and contextual, "the best for that impasse," and emerges in relationship to our previous choices, values, agency, environment, and personal history. God's aim is the "call forward," as John Cobb asserts, inviting us to

---

36   Alfred North Whitehead, *Science and the Modern World* (New York: Free Press, 1967), 192.

align our lives with God's goal for this moment and the immediate and long-term future.

While we seldom fully or directly experience God's vision for this and every moment, we can intuit God's aim through prayer, meditation, study, and personal agency. We can open to God's aim as we "ask, seek, and knock" for greater awareness of God's presence in our lives and the world. We can make the quest for God's vision the heart of personal intentions, conditioning how we experience and respond to the world.

A simple prayer of openness, accompanied by times of quiet contemplation throughout the day, in which we pause to notice God's presence, involves simply asking to experience God's presence in every encounter and moment. Like the young Samuel, we can pray, "Speak God, your servant is listening" or with Brother Lawrence "practice the presence of God" by training our vision to experience the holiness of each moment and creature. Throughout the day, I invoke the words of the Prayer of St. Francis, "Lord, make me an instrument of peace" as a way of attuning myself to God's presence in my inner experience and outer agency.

We can also follow the guidance of Psalm 46, and in the midst of the chaos and busyness of our lives and our communities, pause to "be still" and "know" that God is with us, and in us. The storms may not cease, but when we discover that Jesus is in the boat with us, we will find peace and persistence to ride out the storm, claim our agency to guide the boat through troubled waters, and trust that within the storm, we are guided toward the far shore of justice and peace. (Mark 4:35-41)

Prayer for the Journey. One of the hymns sung at my Ordination into Christian ministry in June 1980 was "O Master, Let Me Walk with Thee," updated in some settings to "O Savior Let Me Walk with You." In that spirit, let this be our prayer.

> *Loving Companion, Guide, and Healer,*
> *Let your realm of love and possibility be incarnate in my life,*

Let me align myself with your vision for this moment,
my lifetime, and the world.
    "O Savior, let me walk with you
In lowly paths of service true
Tell me Thy secret, help me hear
The strain of toil, the fret of care
Teach me thy patience, still with Thee
In closer, dearer company
In work that keeps faith sweet and strong
In truth that triumphs over wrong...
In hope that sends a shining ray
Far down the future's broadening way
In peace that only Thou canst give
With Thee, O Savior let me live." In Jesus' Name. Amen.[37]

---

37   George Washington Gladden, "O Master, Let Me Walk with Thee.

CHAPTER FOUR

JESUS AND THE ONE TO WHOM ALL HEARTS ARE OPEN

> *When Jesus saw her weeping and the Jews who came with her also weeping, he was greatly disturbed in spirit and deeply moved. He said, "Where have you laid him?" They said to him, "Lord, come and see." Jesus began to weep.* (John 11:33-35)

> *But there can be no doubt as to what elements in the [gospel] record have evoked a response from all that is best in human nature. The Mother, the Child, the bare manger: the lowly man, homeless and self-forgetful, with his message of peace, love, and sympathy: the suffering, the agony, the tender words as life ebbed, the final despair: the whole with the authority of supreme victory. I need not elaborate. Can there be any doubt that the power of Christianity lies in its revelation in act, of that which Plato divined in theory?[38]*

As the living embodiment of God's love, Jesus is the Heart of the Universe. The fellow sufferer who understands and the intimate companion who celebrates. He is the friend, celebrated in a hymn of my childhood, "all our sins and griefs to bear." Early Christian theologians asserted that Jesus lived through every season of life from birth to death so that every moment of our lives might be experienced as a holy pathway to God. No doubt Whitehead was aware of the Christmas Carol, "Once in Royal David's City," first published in 1848 as a selection in Cecil Frances Alexander's *Hymns for Little Children,* and now the anchor hymn of King's College, Cambridge, Christmas Eve Festival of Nine Lessons and Carols. As a senior theologian, influenced by the hymns from my Baptist childhood, it is easy for

---
38   Whitehead, *Adventures in Ideas*, 167.

me to imagine Whitehead in his sixties remembering the following words as he pondered God's all-embracing empathy and receptivity.

For he is our childhood's pattern;
Day by day like us he grew,
He was little, weak, and helpless,
Tears and smiles like us he knew:
And he feeleth for our sadness,
And he shareth in our gladness.

To repeat, the Christian vision of divine incarnation proclaims Jesus as the Heart of the Universe, revealing God as the Great Empath and Intimate, "to whom all hearts are open, all desires known, and from whom no secrets are hidden," as the Anglican Book of Common Prayer (1928) affirms. In his table fellowship, healing, relationships, and prophetic words, Jesus reveals God as being both creative and responsive, the source of possibility and the receiver of all value. In his intimate joining of listening and acting, feeling and guiding, we can affirm "Jesus loves me this I know, for the Bible tells me so."

Jesus as the Heart of God. Jesus is fully human and fully divine, according to the great creeds of Christianity. In Jesus' life and ministry, the fully alive one, as Irenaeus describes the glory of God, defines not only what it means to be human but what it means to be divine – growing in wisdom and stature, loving without measure, embracing the wondrous diversity of life, and guiding persons and the planet with wisdom and compassion.

While Christian theologians have never adequately described the dynamics of Jesus' divine-humanity or the nature of God's presence in Jesus' life, at the very least, such affirmations point to Jesus as reflecting fully the incarnation and intentionality of divinity in the affairs of human life, of unity of spirit with God, and as the glory of God, the fully alive person. While many theologians struggled with Jesus' suffering on the cross, believing it contradicted God's eternal perfection, I believe – as did Whitehead – that Jesus' fullest humanity and revelation of God is found in his empathy, suffering, passion, and delight, the emotional availability that gives birth to the call of the realm or kindom of God. An emotionally intimate Jesus reveals an emotionally intimate and personal God contrary to the aloof, impassible, unchanging, and unmoved mover celebrated by the philosopher Aristotle and much of Christian theology. Jesus leads and challenges his followers then and now out of empathy, not apathy; intimacy and not distance; solidarity and not separation; and persuasion not coercion. For Whitehead and – I believe – for Jesus, divine perfection is found in dynamic give and take of relationship and in empathetic embrace and response to the joy and pain of the world.

In the previous chapter, we explored the prophetic call of God in Jesus and saw it as God's active and superjective quest to transform the world. God is the call of the future, urging us to embody justice and peace in our communities and the world. There is also prophetic receptivity. God receives as well as gives: God feels the world in tandem with God's healing action in the world. In describing the prophetic spirit that was later incarnate in Jesus, Abraham Joshua Heschel observes that God reveals Godself:

> in a personal and intimate relationship with the world. He does not simply command and expect obedience. He is also affected by what happens in the world, and reacts accordingly. Events and human actions arouse in Him joy and sorrow, pleasure and wrath...the notion that God can be intimately affected, that He possesses not merely intelligence and will, but also pathos defines the prophetic consciousness of God.[39]

As children, my brother and I were required to learn a Bible verse each week. I recall the verse I recited described Jesus' response to the death of his friend, Lazarus, "Jesus wept." (John 11:35. These two words challenge any theological perspective that privileges apathy over empathy and changelessness over change.

---

39   Abraham Joshua Heschel, *The Prophets: Volume 2* , 3-4.

When Jesus saw her weeping and the Jews who came with her also weeping, he was greatly disturbed in spirit and deeply moved. He said, "Where have you laid him?" They said to him, "Lord, come and see." Jesus began to weep. (John 11:33-35)

God's Chosen One feels pain and grief. God's Beloved Child experiences Mary and Martha of Bethany's pain and joins them in grieving the death of their brother Lazarus. Love listens, grieves, weeps, and responds. Jesus' care is for communities as well as individuals. Jesus feels the pain that comes from injustice and oppression, and the waywardness that leads to destruction. Our politics and citizenship as well as our religion and spirituality matter to God, and Jesus addresses the vital issues of our lives and communities and not just individuals as a companion, friend, and guide.

As Jesus came near and saw the city, he wept over it, saying, "If you, even you, had only recognized on this day the things that make for peace! But now they are hidden from your eyes. Indeed, the days will come upon you when your enemies will set up ramparts around you and surround you and hem you in on every side. They will crush you to the ground, you and your children within you, and they will not leave within you one stone upon another, because you did not recognize the time of your visitation from God." (Luke 19:41)

Our world matters to God and it matters to Jesus. While we cannot construct an entire theology from these two passages, it is clear that the God revealed in Jesus is intimately connected to our world and that the relationship is reciprocal: the God reflected in the life and teachings of Jesus creates and challenges out of relational love and the creaturely world responds to God's challenge and charts its own path, calling forth new possibilities for God to whom all hearts are open and all desires known. God is the ultimate example of the graceful interdependence of life and the Divine Empathy creates an empathetic field of force flowing through all creation.

Whitehead's Divine Companion. In this section we focus on what Whitehead calls the consequent nature of God, the impact of the universe in God's experience as reflective of Jesus' intimacy with the world. God sets the universe in motion with a dream and embeds in all things an Eros toward beauty. The world shapes God's experience, touching God's heart, and inspiring God's involvement as the source of relevant and personal possibility. Indeed, no philosopher has described Divine Receptivity and Suffering Love in greater detail and clarity than Whitehead.

God's consequent nature reflects God's responsive love for the world. Love receives as well as gives. Although Whitehead describes the consequent nature in the prose of a metaphysician, the spirit of God's relationship to the world is breathtaking and passionate in its intimacy and companionship. God is lovingly present in all things as primordial. All things are lovingly received by God as consequent. Certain of God's loving character, faithful through every season, the consequent nature of God "evolves in relationship to the evolving world without derogation to the eternal completion of its primordial nature."[40] Unlimited and constantly growing in vision and experience, God embraces and transforms the world in God's own intimate experience defined by God's creative-responsive love, giving everlasting meaning to the perpetually perishing world.

> The consequent nature is the fluent world become 'everlasting' by its objective immortality in God. Also the objective immortality of actual occasions requires the primordial permanence of the primordial nature of God, whereby the creative advance ever establishes itself endowed with the initial subjective aim [toward beauty, intensity, and complexity for each occasion and the world] derived from the relevance of God to the evolving world.[41]

Inspired by the interdependence of God and the world, Whitehead affirms that "it is as true to say that God is permanent and the World fluid, as that the World is permanent and God is fluid."[42]

---

40   *Process and Reality,* 12.
41   Ibid., 347.
42   Ibid., 347.

God's power, reflected in the life and teachings of Jesus, is relational, not coercive and expansive and not parochial. To invoke the imagery of Celtic Christian spirituality, Jesus is our anamcara, the friend of the soul, precisely because his love is unwavering while his relationships are everchanging. As the author of Lamentations promises, Jesus embodies, and Whitehead describes:

> The steadfast love of the Lord never ceases,
>   his mercies never come to an end;
> they are new every morning;
>   great is your faithfulness. (Lamentations 3:22-23)

You matter to God. You are written on the palm of the divine hand and preserved eternally in God's memory. Never alone or lost in the universe, your life participates in and shapes the moral and spiritual arc of divine artistry. That same promise is given to your friends and family, and enemies and strangers, and to the most minute puff of experience in far off outer space.

> The consequent nature of God is his judgment on the world. He saves the word as it passes into the immediacy of his own life. It is the judgement of tenderness which loses nothing that can be saved. It is also the judgement of a wisdom which uses what in the temporal world is mere wreckage...a tender care that nothing be lost.[43]

Mother (Saint) Teresa counsels, "do something beautiful for God," precisely because God treasures our lives now and forevermore. In the spirit of Jesus and Whitehead, I conclude every "children's sermon" with the affirmation: "God loves you. We love you. You matter and you can do something beautiful for God." This affirmation joins divine affirmation and empathy with human agency.

---

43   Ibid., 346.

Whitehead provides the metaphysics of love that was embodied in his experience of the life of Jesus. The cosmic cosmology of Whitehead is also as intimate as your hopes and dreams.

> The theme of Cosmology, which is the basis of all religions, is the story of the dynamic effort of the world passing into everlasting unity, and the static majesty of God vision, accomplishing its purpose of completion by absorption of the World's multiplicity of effort.[44]

From the vantage point of a prison cell, Dietrich Bonhoeffer asserts that only a suffering God can save. God's power is made perfect, as the apostle Paul preaches, not only in God's grandeur and universality but in God's weakness, God's partnership and solidarity with human suffering and willingness to suffer for our healing. Long before Calvary's cross, God experienced the pain and joy, hope and despair of life, and embraced it as God's own. Jesus is the "fellow sufferer who understands," whose cross points the way to the Heart of God and expands our hearts to embrace the tragic beauty of the world.

> The realm of God is with us today…What is done in the world is transformed into a reality in heaven, and the reality in heaven passes back into the world. By reason of this reciprocal relation, the love in the world passes into the love in heaven and floods back into the world. In this sense, God is the great companion – the fellow sufferer who understands.[45]

Yes, "Jesus loves me, this I know, for the Bible tells me so." In Divine Love, intimacy and cosmology meet, inspiring us to aspire to follow the better angels of our nature as God's companions in healing the Earth.

---

44   Ibid., 349.
45   Ibid., 351.

JUST A CLOSER WALK WITH JESUS

Jesus is the Divine Empath, who shows us the heart of God. God is not aloof and unchanging, unmoved by our joys and sorrows. God is the Heart of the Universe, the most moved mover, the fellow sufferer who understands, and the loving companion who celebrates. God's intimacy is described in Jesus' affirmation that as we have done unto the least of these, we have done unto God. God feels everything that happens from the outside in and the inside out and responds to bring wholeness and beauty of experience in times of pain as well as joy. Jesus is truly our friend, revealing Divine Companionship in the least of these as well as the privileged ones, in sorrow and celebration. In the words of the hymn of my childhood:

> What a friend we have in Jesus,
> all our sins and griefs to bear!
> What a privilege to carry
> everything to God in prayer!
> O what peace we often forfeit,
> O what needless pain we bear,
> all because we do not carry
> everything to God in prayer!
> Have we trials and temptations?
> Is there trouble anywhere?
> We should never be discouraged;
> take it to the Lord in prayer!
> Can we find a friend so faithful
> who will all our sorrows share?
> Jesus knows our every weakness;
> take it to the Lord in prayer![46]

God is near and God is here, and God invites us to see the least of these as God's children and as our kin. In this exercise, begin with reflecting on your relationship with God. What are your joys and

---

46   Joseph M. Scriven, "What a Friend We Have in Jesus."

sorrows? What memories and trauma limit you? About what are you anxious? As the hymn says, "take it to Jesus in prayer." Place these burdens in God's hands either physically by writing them down and placing them in a basket or imaginatively by placing them one by one in Jesus' loving hands.

Expanding on the previous paragraph in your imagination, experience Jesus as your companion. Place your concerns in Jesus' hands. Invite Jesus to carry these with you. In letting go of your concerns, "taking it to God in prayer," you are not giving up your agency, but opening to a wider world of graceful companionship. Bring Jesus' presence to times of challenge and concern: in the hospital waiting room, making life-changing decisions, contemplating ways to respond to injustice. God is with you. God feels your pain and joy. You matter and you are not alone.

In this second practice, open your heart to the world. God invites us to imitate his love for the world. You can, as Martin Luther says, be a little Christ to those whom you meet. You can, in the interplay of Buddhism and Christianity that Whitehead sought, also be a Bodhisattva in training, embracing the pain of the world, responding to need, filled with the Spirit of Compassion. As you watch the news, experience the pain of the world. Experience the pain of the immigrant family on the USA border, the child bullied by classmates, the parent mourning a child killed by gun violence, the fear of change motivating the vitriol of a person wearing a MAGA hat, the terror of a Gazan or Israeli child as bombs drop. See Christ in each of these situations. See Christ in your family and everyone you meet and vow to be an agent of healing and compassion. To paraphrase Mother (Saint) Teresa, do something healing and beautiful for God. Let your life be your gift to God and your neighbor.

One of my favorite spirituals is "Standin' in the Need of the Prayer," which chants, "not my brother, not my sister, it's me, O Lord, standin' in the need of prayer." Let this be your prayer for yourself and others. God, whose heart is open to all creation, who knows me and loves me completely,

I'm standin' in the need of prayer. I bring my joys and sorrows to you. I need your steadfast love and loving companionship. Help me feel you nearby, easing my burdens, and empowering me to ease the burdens of those around me individually and as a citizen. In Jesus' Name. Amen.

CHAPTER FIVE
JESUS AND THE
QUEST FOR PEACE

Blessed are the peacemakers for they will be called children of God. (Matthew 5:9)

Thus peace is the removal of inhibition and not its introduction. It results in a wider sweep of conscious interest. It enlarges the field of attention. Thus peace is self-control at its widest, - at the width where the self has been lost, and interest has been transferred to coordinations wider than personality.[47]

Whitehead – like me – grew up listening to stories of Jesus. No doubt he remembered the story of the storm at sea. (Mark 4:35-41) With thunder crashing and lightning flashing, and their boat tossed like a toy by the waves, the first followers of Jesus lose heart. They fear their lives will be lost until one of them remembers Jesus is asleep in the boat with them. Awakened, Jesus bids the sea, "Peace, be still," and there is a calm. In the midst of chaos, there is a still point, for God is with us. Remembering the metaphysical and theological vision of Divine Love and Companionship articulated by Whitehead, we can boldly affirm with the author of Psalm 46, "Be still and know that I am God…The Lord of hosts is with us. The God of Jacob is with us."

For the philosopher, poet, healer, spiritual guide, and teacher, peace is the gift of recognizing the loving omnipresence and omniactivity of God. Trusting that God is with us, that God treasures our lives, and what we do matters, we can experience the peace that enables us to look beyond self-interest to world loyalty and face the challenges of life with tragic beauty. Peace is not anesthesia, deadening the soul,

---

47   Whitehead, *Adventures of Ideas,* 284.

and constricting our vision. Peace enlarges the soul, enabling us to, like Jesus, "grow in wisdom and stature." (Luke 2:52) In the quest for authentic peace, we discover the wisdom of Jesus' words:

> *For those who want to save their life will lose it, and those who lose their life for my sake will save it. For what does it profit them if they gain the whole world but lose or forfeit themselves?* (Luke 9:24-25)

In letting go of the cramped, anxious, and self-interested self, we discover that we are always in relationship with the Soul of the Universe. Going beyond rugged individualism and possessive nationalism, we become little Christs, mahatmas, and bodhisattvas whose souls embrace the universe, encompassing the Wondrous and Tragic Beauty of Life, and trusting that although our lives perish and that there no guarantees that our vocation of saving the world will succeed, we will be part of God's Holy Adventure forevermore.

Jesus as the Embodiment of God's Peace. Every Christmas, the words of Isaiah are invoked to describe the Incarnate Christ, the Word and Wisdom of God made flesh in Bethlehem and Judea, and now in every land and every heart.

> For a child has been born for us,
> a son given to us;
> authority rests upon his shoulders,
> and he is named
> Wonderful Counselor, Mighty God,
> Everlasting Father, Prince of Peace. (Isaiah 9:6)
> The wolf shall live with the lamb;
> the leopard shall lie down with the kid;
> the calf and the lion will feed together,
> and a little child shall lead them.
> The cow and the bear shall graze;
> their young shall lie down together;
> and the lion shall eat straw like the ox.
> The nursing child shall play over the hole of the asp,

and the weaned child shall put its hand on the adder's
den.
They will not hurt or destroy
on all my holy mountain,
for the earth will be full of the knowledge of the Lord
as the waters cover the sea. (Isaiah 11:6-9)

I believe that Whitehead, like me, heard these words at the lessons
and carols service each Christmas and may have sung to Isaiah 9:6
in Handel's *Messiah*. Having experienced the carnage of war, it is no
mystery that the mature Whitehead sought peace and placed peace
at the heart of his final section of *Adventures of Ideas*. While I cannot
claim to describe fully Whitehead's religious education as a child and
youth, undoubtedly, he pondered the Beatitudes (Matthew 5:1-11),
which I believe are at the heart of Jesus vision of peace, captured
three decades later in the brief saying from John's Gospel: "Peace I
leave with you; my peace I give to you. I do not give to you as the
world gives. Do not let your hearts be troubled, and do not let them
be afraid." (John 14:27)

Blessed are the poor in spirit,
    for theirs is the kingdom of heaven.
Blessed are those who mourn, for they will be comforted.
    Blessed are the meek, for they will inherit the earth.
Blessed are those who hunger and thirst for righteousness,
    for they will be filled.
Blessed are the merciful, for they will receive mercy.
Blessed are the pure in heart, for they will see God.
Blessed are the peacemakers, for they will be called
    children of God.
Blessed are those who are persecuted
    for the sake of righteousness, for theirs is the
    kingdom of heaven.

Blessed are you when people revile you and persecute you
and utter all kinds of evil against
you falsely on my account.
Rejoice and be glad, for your reward is great in heaven,
for in the same way they persecuted
the prophets who were before you.

These countercultural sayings of Jesus are grounded in the affirmation of God's creative-responsive love. God inspires all things and embraces all things. In the storm, we may be anxious, but we can have peace of mind. God's peace is not that of the world which focuses on self-interest and individualism, but in what John Cobb describes as "self-transcending selfhood" and Whitehead counseled as "the width where the self has been lost, and interest has been transferred to coordinations wider than personality."

> *Although Jesus did not present a metaphysical manifesto or systematic ethical system, the words of the Sermon on the Mount* (Matthew 5-7) *describe the pathway to peace through moving from isolated and self-interested individualism and to empathetic and generous globalism and from self-centeredness to God centeredness. In Jesus' vision of peace, there is no "other." No one is alien or outside God's scope of loving empathy. We are all connected, human and non-human, by God's intimate love coursing through all things. Long before Whitehead's vision of an interdependent, intimate universe, woven together by Divine Love, Jesus proclaimed a world in which all humans – and all creatures – are kin and when you do unto the least of these, you shape God's experience.* (Matthew 25:31-46)

You have heard that it was said, "You shall love your neighbor and hate your enemy." But I say to you: Love your enemies and pray for those who persecute you, so that you may be children of your Father in heaven, for he makes his sun rise on the evil and on the good and sends rain on the righteous and on the unrighteous. For if you love those who love you, what reward do you have? Do not even the tax collectors do the same? And if you greet only your brothers and sisters, what more are you doing than others? Do not even the gentiles do the same? Be perfect, therefore, as your heavenly Father is perfect. (Matthew 5:44-48)

Divine perfection, embodied in human life, is the gift of stature, the experience of peace in which our unique and unrepeatable selfhood is joined with the Selfhood of God and the selfhood of all creation. This unity of Spirit expands rather than constricts are personalities. We become more rather than less as we feel the currents of the Divine Empath flowing through our lives and all creatures. Limited though we are, we can embody Irenaeus' vision of "the glory of God as a person fully alive." While we may at times be the "frightened enlightened," our trust is in the fellow sufferer who understands and preserves our lives in God's Holy Adventure. We can be fully alive as we commit ourselves to doing something beautiful for God and our neighbor.

We can let go of our anxieties as a result of our trust in God's omnipresent loving care for us. God's "tender care" is that nothing be forgotten or lost, and in trusting God's care we build our house on the rock of peace and justice.

> *Therefore I tell you, do not worry about your life, what you will eat or what you will drink, or about your body, what you will wear. Is not life more than food and the body more than clothing? Look at the birds of the air: they neither sow nor reap nor gather into barns, and yet your heavenly Father feeds them. Are you not of more value than they? And which of you by worrying can add a single hour to your span of life? And why do you worry about clothing? Consider the lilies of the field, how they grow; they neither toil nor spin, yet I tell you, even Solomon in all his glory was not clothed like one of these. But if God so clothes the grass of the field, which is alive today and tomorrow is thrown into the oven, will he not much more clothe you—you of little faith?... But seek first the kingdom of God and his righteousness, and all these things will be given to you as well.* (Matthew 6:25-30)

As I child, I sang the hymn "Breathe on Me, Breath of God," asking God to "fill me with life anew, that I may love the way you love, and do what you would do." Written in 1878, by Anglican priest Edwin Hatch, Hatch's words might have flowed into Whitehead's consciousness as he pondered the peace that comes from a belief that our lives are eternally treasured in God's consequent nature, God's ever evolving love for the world revealed in the intimacy of God's initial aim.

> Breathe on me, Breath of God,
> so shall I never die,
> but live with you the perfect life
> for all eternity.

In the living Jesus, we experience the inspiration to become peacemakers, whose quest for peace is grounded in our trust that God is with us in all the storms of life. As we seek a better world for ourselves and our kin, we don't have to be afraid of immigrants, those who differ politically from us, or what the future brings for we are forever supported and treasured by God.

Whitehead's Dream of Peace. Alfred North Whitehead concludes his magisterial meditation on Western civilization, *Adventures of Ideas,* with a discourse on peace, joining the Platonic and Galilean visions of the universe and personal life. The movement of history is restless, joining chance, necessity, and force with providence, possibility, and persuasion. The experience of Zest for persons and communities requires novelty and adventure and with novelty and adventure comes loss and conflict. "Decay, Transition, Loss, Displacement belong to the essence of the Creative Advance."[48] Yet, the reality of tragedy haunts every quest for the Realm of God on Earth.

> As soon as high consciousness is reached, the enjoyment of
> existence is entwined with pain. Amid the passing of so much
> beauty, so much heroism, so much daring, Peace is then the

---

48   Whitehead, *Adventures of Ideas,* 286

intuition of permanence. It keeps vivid the sensitiveness to the tragedy; and it sees the tragedy as a living agent persuading the world to aim at fineness beyond what might have been, and was not: What can be. The tragedy was not in vain.[49]

I believe that we can intuit a very personal story beneath Whitehead's cosmological vision and his reflections on peace. Whitehead's vision of peace testifies to the reality of his son Eric's death and his quest to find meaning in the mass slaughter of World War I. Perhaps the seventy-two-year-old philosopher is meditating on the death and maiming of a generation of his students, sacrificed to the God of War, when he notes, "the deepest definition of Youth is, Life as yet untouched by tragedy. And the finest flower of youth is to know the lesson in advance of experience, undimmed. The question here for discussion is how the intuition of peace asserts itself apart from its disclosure in tragedy."[50] Now, seventy-two years of age myself as I pen these thoughts, I am keenly aware of the interplay of innocence and experience, and hope and tragedy.

Even amid tragedy – whether of war or the Cross on Calvary – peace comes from the "surpassing of personality" and the "understanding of tragedy, and at the same time its preservation."[51] This is the countercultural peace that Jesus describes. Jesus and Whitehead see peace as involving the creative transformation of conflict and pain, not the peace of the world. We must choose the Way of the Cross, in whatever form it presents itself to us – the death of a beloved child, protest against terrorist and state sanctioned violence, the decimation of coral reefs and extinction of species by climate change, our own aging and mortality, and the limitations and threats to our cherished institutions – embracing our fear and anxiety, on the hand, and, on the other hand, trusting that our suffering and the suffering of others, and our quest for justice and planetary healing, is treasured eternally by God and will matter to future generations.

49   Ibid., 286.
50   Ibid., 287.
51   Ibid., 285-286.

The Divine Eros, the Energy of Love, that provides the possibilities for civilizational growth and transformation, enables us to see Beauty in tragedy and accept the tragic nature of life as we discover resources for personal and planetary transformation. The expansive soul, refined by both achievement and tragedy, embodies from a finite perspective God's vision of healing and the commitment to cherish, remember, and transform tragedy for the sake of a better tomorrow. There is a Cross on Calvary, in God's heart, and in world history. Beyond the Cross, there is the wondrous mystery of an Empty Tomb and Open Future, filled with ordinary as well as dramatic resurrections, beckoning us beyond the dead ends of life. In embracing the all-encompassing and constantly inspiring Divine Eros and the ever evolving and ever faithful Unity of Adventure, the soul grows in wisdom and stature and becomes God's companion in healing the world.

> At the heart of the nature of things, there are always the dream of youth and the harvest of tragedy. The Adventure of the Universe starts with the dream and reaps Tragic Beauty. This is the secret of the union of Zest with Peace: - That the suffering attains its end in a Harmony of Harmonies. The immediate experience of this Final Fact, with its union of Youth and Tragedy, is the sense of Peace. In this way the world receives its persuasion toward such perfections as are possible for its diverse individual occasions.[52]

JUST A CLOSER WALK WITH JESUS

Jesus promised his followers peace. Not the peace of denial or anesthesia, or the peace of life without challenge. Jesus promised the peace of God's presence which enlivens, enlightens, energizes, and inspires. Peace is the gift of a wider sense of self in which we join our individual self with the Self of the Universe. Peace connects us not only with our past history but the history of the universe in which we are joined with all creation. Pain and death are real, but they are part of a larger history. Our concerns about climate change and the

52   Ibid. 296.

future of our nation's democracy are real and need to be addressed. They are real to God, and God is with us as we address these. Moreover, the perpetual perishing nature of our lives finds completion in God's consequent nature, God's embrace of all things in God's life. This moment and our lives perish and yet live evermore. Nothing can separate us from the love of God who cherishes and preserves our lives eternally and invites us to continue in a holy adventure beyond this lifetime.

In this exercise, feel your connection with the Universe in its fullness. You are a drop in the sea of life, unique and unrepeatable. The Ocean of God's love flows in and through you. Experience your life as part of a never-ending universal journey. You are a child of God, a child of the universe, and your life makes a difference. See yourself emerging from God's love and see your life returning to God's love.

This second spiritual practice is inspired by a Celtic prayer of presence, reminding us that "thin places," transparent to God's presence, are everywhere.

I lie down this night with God,
And God will lie down with me;
I lie down this night with Christ,
And Christ will lie down with me;
I lie down this night with Spirit,
And the Spirit will lie down with me;
God and Christ and the Spirit
Be lying down with me.

During the height of the COVID when persons over sixty-five with health conditions, such as myself, were considered high risk for intubation if they contracted COVID, I was often anxious about my survival. I found peace of mind through visualizing Jesus beside me as I went to sleep each life and as I placed my life in God's care.

As I was writing this text, I was scheduled to take an MRI scan for a possible inner ear tumor. Due to childhood trauma, I am mildly claustrophobic and obsessed about the MRI in the days leading up to the scan. While I was not entirely delivered from anxiety, with a little medicinal help, I made it through the test, visualizing Jesus as my companion in the tube. My recognizing of my anxiety and Jesus' presence in my fears had a positive benefit: once again, I was reminded – thanks to the Great Empath - to feel greater empathy for persons who daily face mental health challenges.

Vietnamese Buddhist teacher Thich Nhat Hanh says peace is every step. Peace is also every breath. On Easter night Jesus surprised his followers by entering the upper room where they secluded themselves, greeting them with the words, "Peace be with you." Then, he breathed on them and said, "Receive the Holy Spirit." In this second exercise, simply breathe, and as you breathe, experience Jesus breathing in and through you. Experience Jesus' peace filling you, inspiring you, and enlightening you. Jesus is as near as your next breath. Experience God's Spirit as your deepest and most intimate reality. Peace is as near as your next breath. Even in your anxiety, Jesus breathes through you, assuring you that you at the heart of God's love and God will neither leave you nor forsake you.

Prayer for the journey. Inspired by another hymn, let us awaken to God's peace. In this prayer of affirmation: Loving Companion, whose light guides me and breath calms me, in your care and presence, I have peace like a river, love like an ocean, and joy like a fountain. Let my peace, love, and joy flow into the world bringing healing and justice, companionship and care, to everyone I meet. In Jesus' Name. Amen.

CHAPTER SIX

THE FUTURE OF JESUS: NEW HORIZONS OF GOSPEL SPIRITUALITY

Very truly, I tell you, the one who believes in me will also do the works that I do and, in fact, will do greater works than these, because I am going to the Father. (John 14:12)

The worship of God is not a rule of safety—it is an adventure of the spirit, a flight after the unattainable. The death of religion comes with the repression of the high hope of adventure… Bolder adventure is needed - the adventure of ideas, and the adventure of practice conforming itself to ideas.[53]

Jesus and Whitehead lived in times of civilizational and spiritual crisis. History was at an inflection point, with the future of humankind in doubt. Jesus lived at the height of the Roman Empire. The resident of an oppressed and occupied land, Jesus never lived for one moment as a politically free person. Hope and fear characterized the daily experience of the peasant class to which Jesus belonged. At any moment, one of the oppressed could be impressed into the service of Rome to do menial labor for the occupation troops. People lived from day to day and hunger was a reality for those who could not catch a day's quota of fish or suffered the impact of drought. Hope was in the air, almost palpable, for the coming of a Messiah, a religious-political leader, who would restore the fortunes of Israel and destroy the Roman Empire. Some sought the coming Messiah through violence, others through prayer, still others in retreat to the mountains and desert. Regardless of a person's Messianic vision, the dream of a new world

---

53   Alfred North Whitehead, *Science and the Modern World*, 192 and *Adventures of Ideas*, 259.

provided a horizon for hope as people faced a difficult and uncertain present and future.

Whitehead lived in a very different world than that of first-century Jesus. Early in his lifetime, Great Britain was at the height of its powers. It was the Empire of its time, ruling land and sea, expansive and colonial in spirit. By the time Whitehead relocated to Harvard University, he had lived through the Boer Wars and World War I. He had seen death firsthand in the premature ending of his son's life and the decimation of a generation of students on the killing fields of Europe. Later in life, from the safe vantage point of Harvard University and Cambridge, Massachusetts, the elder philosopher saw newsreels of German planes bombing London and the atomic bombs wreaking havoc on Hiroshima and Nagasaki and ushering the world into our era of potential mass destruction. During Whitehead's lifetime scientific certainties were in flux as Einstein replaced Newton as the image of scientific adventure. The rapid technological and cultural changes that overwhelm us today were beginning to take shape in the modern world of the 1920s and 1930s. In his long life, Whitehead experienced the devastation of his homeland in World War II, the fall of the British Empire, and the emergence of the American empire. Yet, Whitehead knew the wisdom of the hymn, "Abide with me/Fast falls the eventide." All empires eventually pass. Certainties are outgrown or proven false. The adventures of ideas march on, inviting us toward the New Jerusalem in our ambiguous world.

The savior of Galilee and the philosopher of Cambridge felt the uncertainties and ambiguities of their times. "The hopes and fears of all the years were met" in Jesus' birth and vision of the realm of God and experienced in the academic halls of Harvard. Yet, for both Jesus and Whitehead, history is meaningful, there is a Divine Eros, the dream of the Kingdom of God, reminding us that in the flux and flow of history, there is an evolving movement toward Wholeness, Justice, and Beauty. Jesus proclaimed that the Realm of God, the Commonwealth of Shalom, was in us and among us, arcing toward justice and healing. "Cleave the wood and I am there," proclaims the Gospel of

Thomas' Jesus. Jesus promised his fearful disciples, "I am with you always, to the end of the age." (Matthew 28:20) The Holy Here and Now contains the seeds of a new world order in which humankind lives in peace and all people will experience God's Shalom.

Recently I attended via the internet a conference celebrating the 100th anniversary of Alfred North Whitehead's first classes at Harvard. The conference concluded with a round-table conversation on the Future of Process Philosophy. While the conversation partners affirmed the global impact of process philosophy, they lamented that Whitehead is seldom taught in philosophy departments today. After the flourishing of process theology following World War II and into my generation in the 1970s and 1980s, the same can be said of process theology in the diverse, chaotic, and often metaphysically vapid academic and ecclesiastical theological world of our time, in which only a handful of graduate schools and seminaries regularly offer courses in process theology. The future of Whitehead's vision is uncertain in North America despite its importance in providing a world view for our rapidly changing world, including its growing impact in China.

Similarly, the future of open-spirited visions of Jesus and the church is uncertain. Conservative religious-political forces, fueled by megachurch preachers and multi-billionaires, capture the headlines and exert control over one of the United States' political parties. The Galilean vision of Jesus has been supplanted by the angry voices of politicians, book banning, intentional dishonesty and prevarication, and white Christian and American exceptionalism and nationalism. Christianity has become the vehicle of establishing a mythical Christian nation and the good old days of Christian domination and patriarchy. In some "orthodox" Christian quarters, preaching the Sermon of the Mount can elicit calls of socialism and communism, or the more subtle critique that Christians need to jettison the hospitality and healing ministry of Jesus for hardball "in your face" political power. The power of love, incarnate in Jesus, has been abandoned for the love of power. At the same time, institutional and theological manifestations of progressive and liberal Christianity, once the motive force for the social gospel, human and civil rights, fair economic practices, and peaceful solutions to global conflicts, have been marginalized in the political and cultural sphere. When I introduce myself as a Christian, I often choose to distinguish myself from those who see Christianity as anti-science, anti-LGBTQ+, anti-democracy, anti-intellectual, and anti-pluralism. Yet, as the life of Jesus profoundly demonstrates, the margins can become the frontiers for persons who intuit the moral and spiritual arcs of history and seek novelty to match the novelties of their time. Without an "impossible dream" of God's future realm, and hope in the movements of history toward Wholeness and Beauty, civilization and the planet are doomed to self-destruction. Flickering through it may be, we must have a dream of the future that is motivated by a world order guided by people of stature and compassion for whom world loyalty eclipses the self-interest and the quest for power.

In this section, I ponder the future horizons of the Galilean vision of the first century Jesus in companionship with Whitehead's Jesus-influenced vision. I will be presenting a vision, tentative, fallible, and perhaps too idealistic as well as too narrow. In the spirit of this book, I am inspired by the hymns of faith. Against the forces of death, I find solace in the words of Charles Wesley's "Christ the Lord is Risen Today" and Brian Wren's "Christ is Alive! Let Christian Sing!" Jesus lives! Jesus' message is stronger than the forces of death and destruction, even those perpetrated by those who claim to be the guardians of orthodoxy. Christ is good news! The Galilean vision lives on in our hearts and in the world! Whiteheadian process theology can be an instrument of personal and global transformation for congregations and communities alike.

In the following paragraphs, I will briefly and tentatively chart several possible futures for embracing the Way of Jesus in the context of Whitehead's Galilean vision. I will erect moveable guideposts and not final destinations. My guideposts are meant to be evocative and inspirational, and presentations of areas in which the partnership of Whitehead and Jesus can change the world for the better. In so doing, I will be shaping in a small way the future contours of embodied

Christology as well as Christian process theology. I am writing as a Christian, speaking primarily to Christians, but I am also welcoming pilgrims from other faiths and seekers, the spiritual and not religious, the "nones" and "dones", to be companions on a journey to heal the world. Jesus belongs to the world, not just Christianity, and the Jesus I affirm is at home in an ashram, Zendo, temple, mosque, woodlands, laboratory, library, and any place people seek truth, healing, and community. Christ is, as John Cobb asserts, the way that excludes no authentic ways. In so doing, I seek to embody "the adventure of ideas, and the adventure of practice conforming itself to ideas." Here are twelve images of a Jesus shaped Whiteheadian spirituality for the future.

Ecumenical, Eucharistic, and Evangelical. Deeply influenced by the way of Jesus, the Christian process theology of the future will be holistic, sacramental, and testimonial. The Word and Wisdom of God touches all creation, and revelation and inspiration are present everywhere, challenging us to join tradition and innovation, contemplation and action, intellect and emotion, and prayer and protest in the unfolding of Christianity. In all our diversity, we are one in the Spirit and our diversity, shared creatively and humility, enriches our faith and the world. The way of Jesus in its joining of unity and diversity is revealed in every healthy spiritual temperature from contemplative to Pentecostal. Going beyond the binary and claiming unity amid diversity and diversity amid unity, followers of Jesus can quietly meditate, shout "Hallelujah," speak in tongues, explore the universe, and experience Jesus as their most intimate friend. We can practice a deep ecumenism, honoring the diversity of worship and theological visions within Christianity and open to the insights of other faith traditions as well as seekers and skeptics. Recognizing the need for a robust open-spirited faith, followers of Jesus can share the good news of God's realm and the healing presence of Jesus, without denigrating the wisdom of other faith traditions. We need a "big Jesus," expansive enough to break down the walls of denominational parochialism, economic and racial injustice, and inflexible doctrine and liturgy. Eucharistic in spirit, the universalism of Jesus will see "thin places" everywhere, fostering experiences of the universe as sacramental and embodying Christ's sacramental presence in an economics and politics of affirmation and inclusion, in which we encounter Jesus in the least of these as well as those who presume themselves righteous and privileged. Jesus says to each of us, "you are the light of the world," and Jesus wants us to let our light shine to bring beauty to the world and glory to the Holy One. In Christ's sacramental presence, the one and the many are joined, there is no East or West, but one great community of kinship, including the human and non-human worlds. All places are eucharistic "thin places" revealing God's healing and inspiring love.

Adventurous. Whitehead sees spirituality as inspiring the "high hope of adventure." In the words of the motto of Spain, *Plus Ultra, "there is more" or "further beyond"* describes the future spirit of Christian process theology. Jesus told his disciples to "follow me" and "launch out into the deep." Faith joins stability with innovation, but ultimately calls us to privilege adventure over safety. We can take chances personally and institutionally because God is with us and God treasures eternally our best efforts and uses what we perceive as failure as the steppingstones to personal, institutional, and global transformation. Trusting Jesus' guidance in the labyrinth of life, we can see our lives as a Holy Adventure and embody the closing words of W.H. Auden's Christmas oratorio, "For the Time Being."

> He is the Way.
> Follow Him through the Land of Unlikeness;
> You will see rare beasts, and have unique adventures.
> He is the Truth.
> Seek Him in the Kingdom of Anxiety;
> You will come to a great city that has expected your return for years.
> He is the Life.

Love Him in the World of the Flesh;
And at your marriage all its occasions shall dance for joy.[54]

Mystical. Jesus was a mystic, healer, and prophet, and inspires his followers to embrace a life of transformational intimacy with God.[55] As a child, I felt Jesus as personal and intimate, as near as my next breath and walking beside me on my solitary walks on the banks of the Salinas River. The mystic Jesus invites us to be mystics: to experience unity with God as our deepest reality. To take time for the "sweet hour of prayer" and ground our lives in an intimate give and take with the Divine. While the experience of Holiness is a gift, emerging from God's moment by moment inspiration, described as the "initial aim" by Whitehead, we can "practice the presence of God," as Carmelite Brother Lawrence counsels, by prayer, meditation, visualization, and seeking to experience God in the ordinary as well as the extraordinary, in fixing a child's school lunch as well as gazing at the heavens on a starry, starry night. The church's calling is to transform the world, and one pathway to global transformation is the commitment of the church to become a laboratory of spiritual practices and mystical moments. Mysticism leads to mission and seeking God's realm "on earth as it is in heaven." Awakening to God's moment by moment aim toward beauty and wholeness, harmony and intensity, grounds us in God's vision and takes us from self-interest to world loyalty. God calls us to agency and in our agency, we can join God in healing the world.

Embodied. Among the great religious teachers of the world, Jesus was the most physically oriented. As the Word and Wisdom made flesh, Jesus sought to heal persons in body as well as spirit. In that same spirit, Whiteheadian theology privileges the body as well as the spirit, the physical pole as well as the mental pole, as an object of God's care. Mind and body, and spirit and flesh, flow into one another, and healing the body, transforms the mind; and healing the

54   W.H. Auden, *For the Time Being: A Christmas Oratorio* (Princeton: Princeton University Press, 2013), 136.
55   Bruce Epperly, *Jesus: Mystic, Healer, and Prophet* (Vestal, NY: Anamchara Books, 2023).

mind promotes physical well-being. Bodies matter. God's love can heal cells and souls. God loves the world of bodies of all kinds – black bodies, white bodies, yellow bodies, brown bodies, differently abled bodies, the bodies of our non-human kin, as well as earth, sea, water, and sky. The Christian process theology of the future must focus on the body as inspired and the spirit as embodied in addressing physical well-being, promoting physical and spiritual healing practices, supporting the scientific adventure, especially in medicine, and healing our nation's institutions to improve the health of people around the globe. The embodied theology of the future protests the bombing of innocent people and racist attitudes toward immigrants; it also nurtures healing touch through liturgical laying on of hands, reiki healing touch, and yoga and Tai Chi and various types of energy work. In the spirit of Jesus' healing ministry, joining seamlessly body, mind, spirit, relationships, and community, we join prayer with the promotion of universal health care not only for citizens of our nation but for all the people of the Earth. The healing of persons transforms communities and healthy communities promote health and wholeness among individuals.

Prophetic. Jesus was the child of the prophets, seeking to embody God's realm on earth as it is in heaven. Following the way of Jesus, Christian process theology envisions an alternative world to our current state of violence, incivility, polarization, ecological destruction, and injustice and works to incarnate that world in daily life and the affairs of nations. God's aim in each moment of experience is for the highest values possible for that moment and the world beyond itself. There is a prophetic restlessness, a yearning for the high hope of adventure and civilization of experience, which constantly calls us forward to wider and wider circles of social and political inclusion and well-being. For the Christian process theologian and congregation, God has "skin in the game." What happens in the world matters to God and leaves the world with a greater or lesser impact of God's presence. To do something beautiful for God is to commit to healing the world one moment, relationship, and political policy at a time. Prophetic process theology challenges everything that stands in the way of the realization of abundant life and calls persons and nations to move from self-interest to world loyalty, while recognizing that the God of creative transformation is also present in those who stand in the way of achieving the "more perfect union." Oppressor and oppressed alike are touched by God. Recognizing God's presence in everyone's life, protest can be the pathway to the healing of persons and institutions and not a catalyst for alienation and incivility.

Practical. God is the ultimate idealist. God is also the ultimate realist. Jesus met people where they were in all their wondrous fallibility and conflictedness. Jesus to not enact abstract rules but treated each person in the concreteness of their experience. Each moment of experience is unique. Each situation and person's limitations became the womb of unborn possibilities. Jesus continues to midwife possibilities, working with our imperfections, as he did with Peter, Saul of Tarsus (Paul) Martha, and Mary of Magdala, to bring forth the unique divinity and vocational possibilities of each of us. The interplay of the way of Jesus and Whiteheadian philosophy challenges us to be practical prophets, heavenly minded and earthly good, idealistic and concrete, in addressing the challenges of our time. God's aim is the "best for that impasse" and not an abstract possibility. In daily life and politics, it means looking toward the far horizons of Shalom and mediating the vision of what can be with the realities of what can be achieved in our current situation. We must press forward with eyes on the prize and yet rejoice in each step in realizing the moral and spiritual arcs of history in our lives and the world.

Universalist. John's Gospel, in describing the Cosmic Christ incarnate in Jesus of Nazareth, proclaims:

> All things came into being through the Word and Wisdom of God, and without the Word and Wisdom of God, not one thing came into being. What has come into being in the Word and Wisdom was life, and the life was the light of all people. The light shines in the darkness, and the darkness did not overtake

it…The true light which enlightens everyone, was coming into
the world… And the Word became flesh and lived among us, and
we have seen his glory, the glory as of a God's only Child, full of
grace and truth. (John 1:3-5, 9, 14, author's paraphrase)

The enfleshed Christ, Jesus of Nazareth, is the most personal,
and is also the most universal. Jesus of Nazareth is the infinite God
present in finite time and place. Trusting Jesus, and experiencing Jesus
as personal, opens rather than closes our world. To have a personal
relationship with Jesus, an emotional tie with the Galilean, is to embrace
the personal in all creation. The Christian process theology of the
future sees Jesus as the spiritual guide, healer, teacher, and prophet who
deepens our care for the world in all its wondrous diversity. Friends of
Jesus find Christ's presence in all Holy Paths, not as exceptional but as
invitational, and inspiring us to see Jesus in all his diverse companions
in the quest for personal wholeness and Earth healing.

Personal. The universal is personal in God's revelation in Jesus.
Among liberals and progressives, it is unusual to use the language of
a "personal relationship with Jesus." It seems too individualistic and
private: too reflective of USA individualistic self-interest. Hymns like
"In the Garden" seem to encourage a "Jesus and me" spirituality that
turns its back on our responsibilities to heal the Earth. In contrast,
a process-relational Jesus of the future, joining the Gospel message
and the insights of Whiteheadian cosmology, sees the personal as
global and the global as personal. Process-relational images of Jesus
encourage intimacy with the Living Jesus. When Jewish theologian
and mystic Abraham Joshua Heschel marched with Martin Luther
King, he claimed that "it felt like my legs were praying." The anon-
ymous author of the Russian Orthodox *Way of the Pilgrim* chanted
the Jesus Prayer, "Lord, have mercy upon me a sinner," with every
step and soon experienced Jesus as his closest companion. A deeply
personal Jesus embraces all ways and invites us to see the world with
the eyes of Jesus, asking constantly in the spirit of *In His Steps,* "What
would Jesus do as a citizen, in the context of racism and homophobia,

in the voting booth?" and then listen for Jesus' voice in the words of another hymn of faith, Cecil Frances Alexander, wife of an Irish Anglican bishop, written and published in 1852, and likely known by Whitehead:

> Jesus calls us! O'er the tumult
> of our life's wild restless sea,
> day by day his voice is sounding,
> saying, "Christian, follow me."[56]

God calls us forward in each occasion and moment of experience. We are constantly touched by God's realm of Shalom, even in moments when we are oblivious or turn away from God's vision for us and our communities.

Ecological. The embodied Jesus calls us to become ecological Christians. Long before Francis of Assisi's "Canticle of the Creatures," Jesus saw birds of the air and the grasses of the field praising God. God notes the fall of the sparrow just as God notices us. Jesus inspires a personal relationship with the non-human world, and a Whiteheadian Jesus awakens us to a living, breathing universe, in which creation is touched by God. Faithfulness to Jesus challenges us to be environmental citizens. Although "life is robbery," and our survival depends on consumption, we can "touch the earth lightly," delight in the beauty of the Earth, and join all creation in healing praise and transformational love. God truly loves the world, and feels the world, and what we do in relationship to climate change and species survival matters to the Source of Beauty and Life.

Relational. Relationship is everything. Jesus related personally to everyone from a ritually unclean woman with a flow of blood to a hated tax collector struggling to find meaning in his life. Like the Buddhist bodhisattva, Jesus' heart embraced the universe and mediated healing to all. The Christian process theology of the future is open-hearted as well as open-spirited. Growing in wisdom and stature, we feel the pain of the world, while engaging in practices that deepen our spiritual

56   Cecil Frances Alexander, "Jesus Calls Us Oer the Tumult."

center to face our times seemingly intractable problems. There is no other, nor is the church separated from the life of the world. There is only One World, calling followers of Jesus to be Christ-like wherever they find themselves, whether at home, cheering at a basketball game, hiking with grandchildren, dancing with friends, or making political decisions as citizens or public servants. Followers of Jesus recognize that although governments must engage at times in coercive activities for the public good and national security, our goal should be the peaceful resolution of conflict and to see all people, including undocumented immigrants, political opponents, and international adversaries as God's beloved children, touched by God's aim toward wholeness. There is no "other," alien to us, and this should be the inspiration and challenge of our ecclesiology and politics.

Innovative. In speaking of the realm of God, emerging on the horizon, the prophet Isaiah asserts:

> I am about to do a new thing;
> now it springs forth; do you not perceive it?
> I will make a way in the wilderness
> and rivers in the desert.

Jesus embodies God's novelty in our world, redefining relationships, rules, religion, and the realm of God. Honoring tradition, Jesus also boldly transformed tradition to respond to human need. As the apostle of the moral and spiritual arcs of history, Jesus reveals the Divine Eros calling forth new forms of faith and practice. The worship of God, and alignment with God, is not a rule of safety, to quote Whitehead, but the inspiration embraces the high hope of adventure in religion, culture, science, and politics. The faith of the future is appreciative and innovative, channeling the prayer of Dag Hammarskjold:

> For all that has been – thanks!
> For all that shall be – yes![57]

---

57   Dag Hammarskjold, *Markings* *

Following the way of Jesus, personally and institutionally, means saying "yes" to new dimensions of reality, new images of church, and novel understandings of the spiritual journey. Giving thanks for the past, we sojourn toward the future, aware of our limitations of perspective and history, with eyes on the prize of God's realm of Shalom for all creation.

Hopeful. Langston Hughes challenges us to "hold fast to dreams." Apart from dreams, life is like a bird that cannot fly and a barren frozen field. Jesus was a dreamer and hope giver. Living in an oppressed community, never experiencing a moment of political freedom, Jesus' spirit was nevertheless free and untrammeled. Even on the cross, feeling abandoned, Jesus committed his life to the Reality that overcomes the death-filled machinations of the powers and principalities. Today, we struggle to find hope. We see the decreasing and graying membership of progressive – and now – conservative churches. We fear that we have crossed the threshold in terms of global climate change and can only anticipate ever-escalating species destruction and a barren world for our children and grandchildren. We worry about the survival of democracy and human rights in the "home of the free and the land of the brave." All these fears are realistic and must be addressed. Neither denial nor hopelessness can save us, nor can the false hopes of a constantly updated Second Coming of Jesus. We cannot go on with business as usual, nor can we at the macro level assert that "every little thing's gonna be alright." Still, Jesus claimed that God's realm is in us and among us, growing like a mustard seed, quietly yet persistently. The moral and spiritual arcs energize history and inspire our highest and best efforts to change the world. In words reminiscent of Jesus' description of God's realm, Whitehead describes the immanent hope and challenge of our personal and global history as reflecting the constancy of God's quest for Wholeness and Beauty.

[God's] purpose is always embodied in the particular ideals relevant to the actual state of the world. Thus all attainment is immortal in that it fashions the actual ideas which are God in the world as it is now. Every act leaves the world with a deeper or fainter impress of God. He then passes into his next relation to the world with enlarged, or diminished, presentation of ideal values.[58]

Our hope is that God is with us and that what we do matters now and in eternity, regardless of the outcome of our best efforts at personal, national, and global transformation. Our hope is in the ever-present activity of God in the world, a presence that operates by love and not compulsion and challenges today's followers of Jesus and those who affirm Christian process theology to claim our vocation as God's companions as healers in our complex and uncertain world.

JUST A CLOSER WALK WITH JESUS

In response to the opening words of Fanny J. Crosby's beloved hymn "Blessed Assurance, Jesus is Mine," William Sloan Coffin, it is said to have penned "Blessed Disturber, I am His." I quoted this earlier, because the power of the future and the dream of hope is always disturbing to those who treasure the status quo and the guardians of yesterday's morality and religion, and this disturbance can be felt by progressives as well as conservatives. In the words of Teilhard de Chardin, Jesus embodied "the God of tomorrow," God's realm of Shalom that challenges every personal and political achievement with the vision of God's Peaceable Realm. Jesus calls us to be visionaries of hope, with feet on the ground and dreams of a new world. In this final spiritual practice, take time to quietly reflect on your images of hope:

What gives you hope?

What are the greatest threats to your hopefulness?

Where do you see hope in the world around you?

How can you incarnate hope in your world?

Conclude by a time of silent and prayerful contemplation in which you ask Jesus to show you the way and give you the energy and persistence to embody hope in your world.

---

58   Ibid., 152.

Biblical scholar, organist, mystic, and missionary physician Albert Schweitzer concludes his magisterial *Quest for the Historical Jesus* with the words:

> He comes to us as One unknown, without a name, as of old, by the lakeside, He came to those men who knew Him not. He speaks to us the same words: "Follow thou me!" and sets us to the tasks which He has to fulfill for our time. He commands. And to those who obey Him, whether they be wise or simple, He will reveal himself in the toils, the conflicts, the sufferings which they shall pass through in His fellowship, and, as an ineffable mystery, they shall learn in their own experience Who He is.[59]

Let Schweitzer's words inspire our closing blessing of this text. A process rendering, complementary to Schweitzer's might be:

Jesus comes to us a Holy Mystery and Living Process moving in and through our lives and mysteries as he has done to followers throughout the ages. He comes to us as a surprise and invitation to adventure. In every moment, Jesus calls us to follow and love. Jesus calls us in the challenges and complexities of life and in following Jesus' Way, our hearts, hands, and minds open, and we discover who we are as God's beloved children.

Guide us toward the future, Loving Companion. Let your arc of justice, beauty, and healing flow in and through us that we may claim with humility, compassion, and courage our vocation as your companions in healing the world. In Jesus' Name. Amen.

---

59   Albert Schweitzer, *Albert Schweitzer: The Essential Writings* (Maryknoll, NY: Orbis Books, 2005), 41.

BOOKS TO LIVE BY

Marcus Borg and N.T. Wright, *The Meaning of Jesus: Two Visions.* New York: HarperOne, 2007.

Walter Brueggeman, *Prophetic Imagination.* Minneapolis: Fortress Press, 1978.

John Dominic Crossan, *Jesus: A Revolutionary Biography.* New York: HarperOne 2009.

Daniel Dombrowski, *Process Mysticism.* Albany, NY: SUNY Press, 2023.

Bruce Epperly, *Homegrown Mystics: American Spiritual Visionaries.* Vestal, NY: Anamchara Books, 2024.

_____, *The God of the Growing Edges: Whitehead and Teilhard on Theology, Spirituality, and Social Change.* Gonzalez, FL: Energion Publications, 2024.

_____, *The God of Tomorrow: Whitehead on Metaphysics, Mysticism, and Mission.* Gonzales, FL: Energion Publications, 2024.

_____Healing the World: Whitehead, Francis, Clare, and Bonaventure on Spiritual and Planetary Transformation.* Gonzalez, FL: Energion Publications, 2025.

_____, *Jesus: Mystic, Healer, and Prophet.* Anamchara Books, 2023.

_____, *Mystics in Action: Twelve Saints for Today.* Maryknoll, NY: Orbis Books, 2020.

_____, *The Mystic in You: Discovering a God-filled World.* Nashville: Upper Room Books, 2018.

_____, *Process Theology: A Guide for the Perplexed*. London: Continuum, 2011.

_____, *Process Theology and Mysticism*. Gonzales, FL: Energion, 2024.

_____, *Process Theology and Politics*. Gonzales, FL: Energion, 2020.

_____, *Process Theology and Prophetic Faith*. Gonzales, FL: Energion, 2024.

_____, *Process Theology: Embracing Adventure with God*. Gonzales, FL: Energion, 2014.

Heschel, Abraham Joshua, *The Prophets*. Peabody, MA: Hendrickson, 2007.

Lowe, Victor, *Alfred North Whitehead: The Man and His Work*. Baltimore: Johns Hopkins Press, 1985.

Whitehead, Alfred North. *Adventures of Ideas*. Paperback. New York: The Free Press, 1933.

_____, *The Function of Reason*. Boston: Beacon Press, 1969.

_____, Mathematics and the Good" and "Immorality," *The Philosophy of Alfred North Whitehead: Library of Living Philosophers*, volume 3, Paul Arthur Schilpp, editor. Evanston, IL: Northwestern University Press, 1941

_____, *Modes of Thought*. New York: The Free Press, 1968.

———. *Process and Reality: Corrected Edition*. Edited by David Ray Griffin and Donald W. Sherburne. New York: The Free Press, 1979.

_____, *Religion in the Making*. New York: Meridian, 1960.

_____, *Science and the Modern World*. New York: Free Press, 1967.

www.ingramcontent.com/pod-product-compliance
Lightning Source LLC
LaVergne TN
LVHW041206080426
835508LV00008B/820